INSIDE THE ASYLUM

INSIDE THE ASYLUM

Why the UN and Old Europe Are Worse Than You Think

JED BABBIN

Since 1947
REGNERY
PUBLISHING, INC.
An Eagle Publishing Company • Washington, DC

Library of Congress Cataloging-in-Publication Data on file with the Library of Congress

ISBN 0-89526-088-3

Published in the United States by
Regnery Publishing, Inc.
An Eagle Publishing Company
One Massachusetts Avenue, NW
Washington, DC 20001

Visit us at www.regnery.com

Distributed to the trade by
National Book Network
4720-A Boston Way
Lanham, MD 20706

Printed on acid-free paper
Manufactured in the United States of America
10 9 8 7 6 5 4 3 2 1

Books are available in quantity for promotional or premium use. Write to Director of Special Sales, Regnery Publishing, Inc., One Massachusetts Avenue, NW, Washington, DC 20001, for information on discounts and terms, or call (202) 216-0600.

I dedicate this book to an unknown American. I saw this man only for a moment on September 11, 2001. The television crews massing near the fallen World Trade Center were interviewing everyone who came within range of their microphones. Clad in blue jeans and a T-shirt, topped by a construction worker's hard hat, the man was walking purposefully toward the disaster. When the reporter asked him, "What are you going to do when you get there?" he looked ahead and replied, "Whatever they need me to do." That man and millions of other Americans just like him are the strength of this great nation.

CONTENTS

CHAPTER ONE

WELCOME TO THE ASYLUM

"The UN is now a central problem for the world, because we take too much notice of it."

—British historian Paul Johnson

IF THE DEMOCRATIC PARTY OF JOHN KERRY AND HILLARY CLINTON HAS its way, UN secretary-general Kofi Annan and French president Jacques Chirac will hold a veto over American foreign policy. The Kerry-Clinton Democrats believe that America's national security and foreign policy should be made subservient to the United Nations and Old Europe in the name of "multilateralism." Gone will be George W. Bush's decisive "unilateral" defense of American interests. Instead, we will have multilateral inaction, terrorism treated as a matter for the police and the courts, and our own foreign policy dictated by the UN and the elites of Old Europe. We've been down this road before, during the presidency of Bill Clinton—and we learned that it leads to failure. It leads us farther from security for our nation, and farther from victory against terrorists and the nations that support them.

One definition of insanity is doing the same thing, in the same way, over and over again and expecting different results. In the asylum that the United Nations has become, this form of insanity is not suffered by all the inmates. The most severe cases are the democratic countries that always want to give the UN another chance to be what it was supposed to be: a forum for nations of good will to meet and settle disputes peacefully without resort to war. Instead, today's UN is a diplomatic version of the Mad Hatter's tea party, where good is evil, right is wrong, and every dictator and despot is given the same rights and privileges as the leaders of free nations. For the United States, the UN is a quagmire of diplomacy in which wars can be lost but not won, alliances can dissolve but not be formed, the birth of nuclear terrorism is being watched but not aborted, and no adult supervision is imposed on a Third World playground where anti-Americanism is the favorite game.

The UN General Assembly is a gaggle of has-beens and never-wases that believes raiding the U.S. Treasury is its right. The Security Council—supposed to be the strongest force for peace—is interested only in tying down the world's remaining superpower, the United States, and making any American action taken without UN permission illegitimate in the eyes of the world.

President Bush's policy of preempting terrorists—attacking them before they can attack America—depends on more than the superiority of American arms. It depends on surprise, hitting terrorists where they lurk before they have a chance to run. That means the UN is the enemy of preemption. Every time we engage in endless, pointless UN debates, we give up the crucial advantage of surprise. The terrorists know that, and so do our so-called "allies" in Europe.

America and its real allies have toppled two terrorist regimes in spite of the UN, not because of it. If American foreign policy were subordinated to the judgment of the Security Council, the Taliban would be negotiating from its stronghold in Kabul, Saddam would still be in power in Iraq, and the threat of al-Qaeda would be tolerated as the cost of doing business in the twenty-first century. The UN can't aid the fight against terror because its members—in thrall to the rogue nations among them—can't even agree what terrorism is. The UN has become a tool for outlaw nations, their European trading partners, and the tin-pot dictators of the world to constrain American action everywhere, especially in the global war against terrorism. By delaying justice and denying its approval to the forces of good in the fight against evil, the UN functions as a shield for the enemies of freedom.

As I'll show later on, the UN isn't content with its Lilliputian attempts to tie down the American Gulliver. It is also an errand boy for the despots of the world. The UN not only turns a blind eye to terrorism, but is actually quite comfortable with it, admitting terrorists to the community of nations, tolerating their development of nuclear weapons, and—in at least one of its largest agencies—putting members of terrorist organizations on its payroll.

Hezbollah—the terrorist organization that has more American blood on its hands than any other except al-Qaeda—is entrenched adjacent to UN "peacekeeper" bases on the Israeli-Lebanese border. On page 155, there is a picture taken from an Israeli Defense Force position called Post Tziporen. The picture shows something Israelis see every day, but the media and the world ignore: two flagpoles about fifteen feet apart; on one, the blue UN flag, and on the other, the yellow flag of Hezbollah, bearing an AK-47 assault rifle held in a clenched fist.

An Israeli soldier who served at that IDF post in 2003 described to me what he saw there, how the UN and Hezbollah men go about their daily routines side by side. The Hezbollah—identified by the uniforms and ski masks they wear—use the same telephones, drink the same water, and get along quite nicely with the UN "peace monitors." At Post Tziporen, UN tolerance of terrorism is visible to the naked eye. But this is only one small part of the problem. The UN's tolerance of—and even support for—terrorism is embedded in the minds of all, from the lowliest "peacekeepers" to the highest appointed officials. This acceptance is insidious and pervasive.

Tolerance of terrorism is only one of the UN's unstated noxious norms. Another is financial corruption. The UN's Oil-for-Food program was supposed to allow Saddam Hussein's Iraq to sell oil only for food and medicine to supply the needs of the Iraqi people. But the corruption of the UN allowed Saddam to skim billions of dollars to buy arms, to buy UN Security Council votes, and to bribe politicians and UN officials at the highest levels. Under the UN's supervision, even the small portion of money truly spent on medicine and food was wasted. Much of the food wasn't even, in the words of one program investigator, "fit for pigs."

The UN is not only financially corrupt, but is also morally and intellectually so. During the Iraq campaign, beginning in March 2003, there was, all too often, graphic proof of Iraqi abuse, torture, and murder of American prisoners of war. Did UN secretary-general Kofi Annan condemn Iraq for these atrocities? No. About a week into the war, he admonished *both sides* to treat prisoners of war humanely. Annan's perverse moral relativism is but a symptom of the disease infecting both the UN and Old Europe.

Our national security will be greatly reduced—and our foreign policy chained to false friends and true enemies—if the UN and Old Europe again annex American foreign policy through the tool of the Democratic Party. As former UN ambassador Jeane Kirkpatrick told me, "The issue is whether the UN should have any role in U.S. decisions on the use of force." She added, "There is no ground in the UN Charter or in precedent to support the position that the Security Council is the only source of legitimacy for the use of force.... The importance of American sovereignty over American action is of the utmost importance." According to Ambassador Kirkpatrick, "We must never agree that the U.S. needs the permission of the Security Council or any non-American entity to take action to protect our security. That is an irreducible responsibility and obligation of our government, which of course is responsible to the Congress and the American people as specified in our Constitution."

For the UN to be an arbiter of legitimacy, it would have to first be able to distinguish between right and wrong, between good and evil. But its charter and its membership preclude that. How can any group granting the worst despotisms in the world and the freest and greatest democracies the same standing and rights be a judge of right and wrong? The UN, by its charter, equates Syria with the United States, China with Britain, and the Sudan (where chattel slavery is still practiced) with Israel. What Kofi Annan and the UN demand is that the legitimacy of the decisions and actions of free nations be dependent upon the approval of the despotisms. It is a fraud on the world, and will continue as long as we tolerate it.

What the United States needs to do is reform its alliances to fit reality, rather than the past, and end its membership in the UN. The nations of the West are no longer united by the threat of Soviet expansionism, and the emasculated nations of Old Europe—the EUnuchs—have sunk to a level of decadence unseen since the 1930s. Europe's core values concerning morality, freedom, and defending the West have diverged from where we as Americans stand. Old Europe has returned to a policy of appeasement, refusing to see the threats being born around it, and choosing to abandon the military capacity to deal with them. Old Europe sees America only as an obstacle to its own economic growth, and as a danger to its elegant diplomacy of inaction. While Americans shed blood to fight terrorism, the shopkeepers of Old Europe make special trade deals with terrorist nations.

France, the self-appointed leader of Old Europe, challenges American action on every economic, diplomatic, and military front in order to support its false claim to global power. France is not a global power. It only plays one on television and in the UN. Those who follow France's leadership—Germany, Belgium, and the others who flock to the banner of the European Union—are allying themselves to thwart American decisions in the UN, in NATO, and in the diplomatic fight against such terrorist-sponsoring states as Iran, Syria, and Saudi Arabia.

Given Old Europe's cowardice and greed, NATO's usefulness might be over. And so is the usefulness of the UN.

After the fall of Saddam Hussein—accomplished only because America finally lost patience with the UN—America's crisis of confidence in the UN has grown acute. The Security Council, having passed seventeen resolutions seeking Saddam's disarmament, was utterly incapable of doing what the UN Charter says it should: enforce its resolutions to keep the peace. If the UN cannot be relied upon to fulfill its own purpose, why should American taxpayers spend more than $7 billion *every year* to sustain it?

Even UN secretary-general Kofi Annan knows that something has to give. In September 2003, he told the Security Council, "Excellencies, we have come to a fork in the road. This may be a moment no less decisive than 1945 itself, when the UN was founded." This book will demonstrate that America, too, is at a crossroads. And the path we need to take leads us out of the UN.

CHAPTER TWO

THE UN: HANDMAIDEN OF TERRORISM

"The Security Council decides that all States shall...refrain from providing any sort of support...to entities...involved in terrorist acts..., take the necessary steps to prevent the commission of terrorist acts..., [and] deny safe haven to those who finance, plan, support or commit terrorist acts."

—UN Security Council Resolution 1373, passed in response to the September 11, 2001, attacks on the United States

BY SIGNING THE UN CHARTER, EVERY MEMBER NATION AGREES TO accept and carry out the resolutions of the Security Council.[1] But the democracies of the world are the only members that ever do. In fact, even UN agencies trusted to carry out the resolutions usually either ignore them or work to violate them. The best example is the UN's nuclear watchdog, the International Atomic Energy Agency (IAEA).

The UN as Midwife to the Birth of Nuclear Terrorism

Mohamed ElBaradei is the UN's head of the IAEA. The agency is supposed to inspect atomic energy programs to make sure they don't violate bans on nuclear weapons proliferation. But like his boss, Secretary-General Kofi Annan, ElBaradei is willfully blind to the facts.

Ever since the radical Islamic takeover in 1979, Iran has been fever-ishly working to produce nuclear weapons, all the while denying and concealing its intent and its work. At a November 2003 *American Spectator* dinner, Undersecretary of State John Bolton took the IAEA to task:

> To date, three reports by...the International Atomic Energy Agency have established that Iran is in violation—in multiple instances—of its safeguards obligations under the Nuclear Non-Proliferation Treaty. While Iran has consistently denied any program to develop nuclear weapons, the IAEA has amassed an enormous amount of evidence to the contrary that makes this assertion increasingly implausible.
>
> After extensive documentation of Iran's denials and deceptions over an eighteen-year period, and a long litany of serious violations of Iran's commitments to the IAEA, the [latest IAEA] report nonetheless concluded that "no evidence" had been found of an Iranian nuclear weapons program. I must say that the report's assertion is simply impossible to believe. This is not only the administration's view. Thomas Cochran, a scientist with the Natural Resources Defense Council, told the *New York Times* that "it's dumbfounding that the IAEA, after saying that Iran for eighteen years had a secret effort to enrich uranium and separate plutonium, would turn around and say there was no evidence of a nuclear weapons program. If that's not evidence, I don't know what is." Gary Samore, a former Clinton administration official now with the International Institute of Strategic Studies in London, told the *London Telegraph* that "this is unquestionably a bomb program."

The United States believes that the massive and covert Iranian effort to acquire sensitive nuclear capabilities makes sense only as part of a nuclear weapons program. Iran is trying to legitimize as "peaceful and transparent" its pursuit of nuclear fuel cycle capabilities that would give it the ability to produce fissile material for nuclear weapons. This includes uranium mining and extraction, uranium conversion and enrichment, reactor fuel fabrication, heavy water production, a heavy water reactor well suited for plutonium production, and "management" of spent fuel—a euphemism for reprocessing spent fuel to recover plutonium. The recent IAEA report confirms that Iran has been engaged in all of these activities over many years, and that it deliberately and repeatedly lied to the IAEA about it.

The international community now has to determine whether Iran has come clean on this program and how to react to the large number of serious violations to which Iran has admitted.... If it is continuing to conceal its nuclear program and has again lied to the IAEA, the international community must be prepared to declare Iran in noncompliance with its IAEA safeguards obligations.[2]

Bolton's proofs are conclusive: The IAEA is blind because it refuses to see. Because the IAEA refuses to see, the reality of a nuclear-armed Iran grows closer every day, and with it grows the danger of nuclear terrorism.

Last year, a delegation from the European Union—hoping to avert a diplomatic crisis between the United States and Iran, and anxious to befriend Iran for its oil—negotiated an expanded inspection plan for Iran's nuclear program. Under this agreement, Iran promised to allow IAEA inspectors unfettered access to its nuclear facilities, along the lines of the "anywhere, any time" no-notice inspections that Saddam Hussein's regime agreed to in the 1991 cease-fire closing the first Gulf War. But, just as Saddam before them, the Iranians immediately reneged on the deal. And both the IAEA and the EUnuchs remain content with this sort of "progress."

While the IAEA closes its eyes to Iran's nuclear weapons program, its director general is more interested in the "security deficit" he sees between the nuclear haves and the have-nots. In a February 12, 2004, op-ed in the *New York Times*, ElBaradei wrote:

> [A] fundamental part of the non-proliferation bargain is the commitment of the five nuclear states recognized under the non-proliferation treaty—Britain, China, France, Russia and the United States—to move toward disarmament. Recent agreements between Russia and the United States are commendable, but they should be verifiable and irreversible. A clear road map for nuclear disarmament should be established—starting with a major reduction in the 30,000 nuclear warheads still in existence, and bringing into force the long-awaited Comprehensive Nuclear Test Ban Treaty....
>
> We must also begin to address the root causes of insecurity. In areas of longstanding conflict like the Middle East, South Asia, and the Korean Peninsula, the pursuit of weapons of mass destruction—while never justified—can be expected as long as we fail to introduce alternatives that redress the security deficit. We must abandon the unworkable notion that it is morally reprehensible for some countries to pursue weapons of mass destruction yet morally acceptable for others to rely on them for security—and indeed to continue to refine their capacities and postulate plans for their use.

To ElBaradei, there is no difference between American or British possession of nuclear weapons and North Korea's possession of them. The greatest threat of the use of nuclear weapons comes—directly and indirectly—from terror-sponsoring states such as Iran. Iran's leaders have announced that obtaining nuclear weapons is—to them—a religious obligation. Defense sources told me that Iran might already have three nuclear weapons purchased from former Soviet satellite states. Iranian missiles—a substantial number of them highly capable Scud derivatives that could be mated to nuclear weapons—can reach most of the Middle East and soon will have the ability to reach all of Europe, even as far as the United Kingdom.

Iran supports many of the most dangerous terrorist organizations, including Hezbollah and other regional terrorist bands, but most important is its alliance with al-Qaeda and global terrorism. Iran admits that several al-Qaeda leaders are in Iran, but it won't surrender them to face justice because its goals and values are those of the terrorists. Once it can, Iran will arm terrorists with nuclear weapons, and then it is only a matter of time until one is smuggled into the United States and detonated, causing hundreds of thousands of casualties. If we suffer a nuclear September 11, al-Qaeda and its Iranian allies will almost certainly have carried out the attack.

The Iranian mullahs have already said that if they had nuclear weapons, they would use them on Israel. In 1981, Israeli aircraft knocked out Saddam Hussein's nuclear program in the Osirak raid. But Iran's nuclear programs are, according to intelligence sources, dispersed among several sites—some of them hardened and underground—that aren't susceptible to such an attack.

If the IAEA—and the EU—joined the U.S. to create an international consensus to compel Iran to surrender its nuclear program, there is a remote possibility that the mullahs would comply. But in the absence of that consensus, the only defense against Iran's nuclear arms program is American action, which needs to include unrelenting diplomatic and economic pressure, and serious covert operations to topple the mullahs' regime. We cannot afford to wait for the IAEA to act, because the IAEA merely reflects the corruption of the UN.

The UN as a Base of Operation for Terrorists in the United States

UN delegations themselves are a constant source of concern. In June 2002, two Iranian "diplomats" were caught casing the Statue of Liberty and were expelled.[3] The statue is one of the announced targets of al-Qaeda. In November 2003, two more Iranians working for the Iranian UN mission were caught videotaping a New York subway in Queens, New York, and also were expelled.[4] Many foreign diplomats use their American UN base to conduct espionage activities in the United States.

Case in point: On November 19, 2002, the Benevolence International Foundation (BIF) was designated a terrorist organization by the U.S. Treasury Department.[5] Apparently founded by Mohammed Jamal Khalifa, a brother-in-law of Osama bin Laden, the BIF moved its headquarters to the United States in March 1992.[6] In the 1990s, it operated in Bosnia under the name of Bosanska Idealna Futura, funneling money and munitions to al-Qaeda and other terrorists. Enaam Arnaout, its director, was later indicted in the United States for terrorist activities.

According to Global Information Systems, an intelligence and news analysis organization, when Huso Zivalj became Bosnia-Herzegovina's ambassador to the United Nations in January 2001, he secretly and illegally gave special UN status to Saffet Catovic in New York, giving him a yellow UN pass. (Red passes are for attachés and other diplomats, up to first secretary; yellow is reserved for the ambassador, permanent representative, or deputy permanent representative.) This allowed Catovic free access to the UN buildings. Zivalj kept this information secret, largely because it was illegal.[7]

According to Steve Emerson of The Investigative Project, Catovic quickly became one of the BIF's spokesmen and fund-raisers,[8] and even lectured at a "jihad camp" in Pennsylvania.[9]

Evan Kohlmann, senior terrorism consultant for The Investigative Project, summed it up this way:

Throughout the 1990s, various international terrorist organizations were able to manipulate UN agencies and resources around the world in order to support their...goals. Some of these international diplomatic bodies, including even the United Nations headquarters in New York, have been infiltrated by known supporters of terrorism—who...provided tactical information to a terror cell targeting that very same complex in 1994. Similarly, foreign intelligence officers masquerading as UN diplomats have been able to use their status of immunity to conduct reconnaissance on other potential terrorist targets in the northeast.

Espionage activities in the UN are nothing new, and the UN's tolerance of espionage and terrorism is old and systemic, and includes granting "observer" status to Yassir Arafat's Palestinian Authority, which is encouraged, in the words of the UN, "to participate as observers in the sessions and the work of the General Assembly" and to maintain "permanent offices at [UN] Headquarters." Terrorists, to the UN, are acceptable UN observers because terrorism, to the UN, is not easily defined; it is in the eye of the beholder.

The UN's Free Pass to Terrorists

The UN's Counter-Terrorism Committee is composed of the entire Security Council. It was created by Resolution 1373 on September 28, 2001.[10] The resolution requires all UN member states to deny support to terrorists, to cooperate in finding and arresting them, and generally sets out the terms with which terrorism should be dealt. But it doesn't define what terrorism is, because the UN can't agree. And that makes the resolution—and its requirements—virtually meaningless.

As Israel's ambassador to the United States, Daniel Ayalon, told me, "Right now, in the International Court of Justice," there is an attempt "to bring Israel to trial because of certain self-defense measures we have to take, because of the [Palestinian terrorist] attacks. But they [the International Court of Justice] will not try terrorism, specifically suicide bombing, which I think is the plague of our time. And why not?

Because it's outside their jurisdiction. You cannot try anybody in international courts for terrorism. You know why? Because they can't even define terrorism."

Ayalon continued, "You come to this body—the UN—which is supposed to be the lightning rod for morality, [and yet] you cannot pass a resolution or find a definition for terrorism." He added, "When there was an attempt to have a very short, objective definition—with no political connotations attached—you will not have that because the Arab countries will not have that pass."

The UN debate on defining terrorism hasn't established anything other than a convenient excuse for inaction. Some states—and non-states, such as the Palestinian Authority—insist that the definition exclude attacks on military targets, which is absurd. Under that definition, the September 11, 2001, attack on the Pentagon wasn't terrorism.

Actually, defining terrorism is easy. All the UN had to do was adopt the definition of terrorism that is already implicit in international law: The Geneva Convention defines a "lawful combatant" and—by exclusion—defines terrorism.

Under the Geneva Convention for the Treatment of Prisoners of War, the major nations that comprise the UN Security Council have agreed on those who are "lawful combatants"—that is, those who are entitled to protection as prisoners of war. The definition of lawful combatants includes, among others, those who are:

- Members of the armed forces of a party to the conflict, including militias or volunteer corps forming part of such armed forces
- Members of other militias and members of other volunteer corps, including those of organized resistance movements, belonging to a party to the conflict and operating in or outside their own territory, provided that they fulfill the following conditions: First, being commanded by a person responsible for his subordinates, second, having a fixed dis-

tinctive sign recognizable at a distance, third, carrying arms openly, and fourth, conducting their operations in accordance with the laws and customs of war.

- Members of regular armed forces who profess allegiance to a government or an authority not recognized by the detaining power
- Persons who accompany the armed forces without actually being members thereof, such as civilian members of military aircraft crews, war correspondents, supply contractors, members of labor units or of services responsible for the welfare of the armed forces, provided that they have received authorization from the armed forces which they accompany
- Members of crews of the merchant marine and the crews of civil aircraft of the parties to the conflict
- Inhabitants of a non-occupied territory, who on the approach of the enemy spontaneously take up arms to resist the invading forces, without having had time to form themselves into regular armed units, provided they carry arms openly and respect the laws and customs of war[11]

Terrorists fail to meet almost all of these criteria and thus are not protected by the Geneva Convention. They are, therefore, outlaws under the law of war. By refusing to use the definition that already exists, the Security Council is blocking any UN action against terrorism. And by creating that obstacle, the UN makes a peaceful solution to terrorism much less likely.

If the UN agreed on a definition for terrorism—and thereby created a basis for deciding which nations are terrorist nations—it could take peaceful action against terrorist states through economic sanctions such as trade embargos, restrictions on the transfer of funds, and restrictions on the free movement of people from terrorist states. Short of such international action—which the UN won't take because terrorism is practiced and supported by several UN members—war becomes the only option.

Defining terrorism is not an academic exercise. Moqtadr Sadr, a minor Shiite cleric, has ordered his terrorist "militia" to kill Americans in Iraq. When the U.S.-led coalition forced Sadr's "newspaper" to stop publishing, Senator John Kerry said, "They shut a newspaper that belongs to a legitimate voice in Iraq...Well, let me...change the term 'legitimate.' It belongs to a voice—because he has clearly taken on a far more radical tone in recent days and aligned himself with both Hamas and Hezbollah, which is a sort of terrorist alignment." If direct alliance with Hamas and Hezbollah—in addition to being funded by Iran, which Sadr is—is only "sort of" a terrorist alignment in Kerry's viewpoint, what could Sadr possibly do to qualify himself as a terrorist? We'll never learn that answer from the UN.

Part of the reason, of course, is the sheer moral relativism of the UN. But another part is the UN's long love affair with Yassir Arafat and Palestinian terrorism.

Yassir Arafat: The UN's Favorite Terrorist

On November 13, 1974, Arafat addressed the UN General Assembly for the first time. "The old world order is crumbling before our eyes," he said, "as imperialism, colonialism, neo-colonialism and racism, the chief form of which is Zionism, ineluctably perish." Arafat said he was a "revolutionary;" his opponents were the "terrorists":

The difference between the revolutionary and the terrorist lies in the reason for which each fights. For whoever stands by a just cause and fights for the freedom and liberation of his land from the invaders, the settlers, and the colonialists, cannot possibly be called terrorist, otherwise the American people in their struggle for liberation from the British colonialists would have been terrorists; the European resistance against the Nazis would be terrorism, the struggle of the Asian, African, and Latin American peoples would also be terrorism, and many of you who are in this Assembly hall

were considered terrorists... As to those who fight against
the just causes, those who wage war to occupy, colonize,
and oppress other people, those are the terrorists. Those are
the people whose actions should be condemned, who should
be called war criminals: for the justice of the cause deter-
mines the right to struggle.[12]

To insist, as the UN has done for thirty years, that Arafat and the
Palestinian Authority are not themselves terrorists is simply to perform
for them the same service that the IAEA is performing for Iran. According to an excerpt I saw from a confidential Israeli report, there have
been more than nineteen thousand attacks on Israelis since Arafat's
intifada began in September 2000: more than twenty-five a day.
According to that report, almost nine hundred Israelis have been killed,
and nearly six thousand wounded in the terrorist attacks.

In October 2003, I interviewed Ziad abu Ziad, a senior advisor to the
Palestinian Authority and formerly its "minister of state." Ziad is an educated man. Well dressed and well spoken, he is a Westernized face of terrorism. We spoke at length about the 1993 Oslo Accords, under which
the Palestinians promised to end their acts and support of terrorism.

Ziad refers to terrorists as "activists"—a moral equivalency that the
UN, because of its large membership of unsavory Third World dictatorships, and Old Europe, because of its hunger for Arab oil, too often
accept. He and the other Palestinians I met with accept no responsibility for the failure of the Oslo Accords. He bragged—falsely—that from
about 1996 to 2000, the Palestinian Authority ended terrorism. I asked
Ziad why it didn't do so now. "Because we didn't get anything for it,"
he told me. For Ziad and Arafat, the destruction of Israel is the goal
and terrorism is the tool.

A host of terrorist organizations—including Hezbollah, Hamas,
Islamic Jihad and Arafat's own Al-Aqsa Martyrs' Brigade—work with
and through the Palestinian Authority. Photographs and documents
seized by the Israeli army during its 2002 incursion into Arafat's

Ramallah compound showed that Saddam Hussein was funding terrorism against Israel through the Palestinian Authority. Money to support Palestinian terrorist activities was also donated by Iran, Syria, and Saudi Arabia.[13] Most of the financial transactions were performed through the Arab Liberation Front and the Palestinian Liberation Front, headed by Abu al-Abbas, the same man who was briefly the Palestinian "prime minister."[14]

Among the documents the Israelis found were copies of checks paid through the Palestinian Authority to the families of the terrorist bombers. Typical, in the words of the Israeli report, is a check for $25,000, drawn on the Palestinian Investment Bank, payable to "Khaldiya Isma'il Abd al-Aziz al-Hurani, the mother of Hamas terrorist Fuad Isma'il Ahmad al-Hurani, who carried out a suicide attack on 9 March 2002 in the *Moment* café in Jerusalem. 11 Israelis were killed and 16 wounded in the attack."[15]

Separating "mainstream" Palestinian organizations from terrorist groups is impossible. In 2003, the United States imposed a requirement that Palestinian non-governmental organizations (NGOs) certify that none of the money they received would be passed through to terrorists. According to a statement by Azmi al-Shuabi, the chairman of the Palestinian economics affairs committee, Palestinian NGOs received about $30 million in 2003 from USAID alone. They all refused to sign the certification.[16]

The UN doesn't even try to make such distinctions, because it believes that money given by Saddam Hussein, Syria, Iran, and Saudi Arabia to Palestinian suicide bombers was and is money given to a just cause.

The UN's Salaried Terrorists

The UN's High Commissioner for Human Rights is supposed to "lead the international human rights movement by acting as a moral authority and voice for victims."[17] Ireland's Mary Robinson was the commissioner from 1997 to 2002. She set the tone for UN dealings with Palestinian terrorism by telling the world that their cause was just, so their methods were to be excused. Under Robinson, the UN Human Rights Commission sanctioned the use of "all available means" to fight Israel.[18]

The UN Relief and Works Agency for Palestinian Refugees in the Near East (UNRWA) is under the control of the high commissioner. UNRWA bills itself as "the main provider of basic services—education, health, relief, and social services—to over 4.1 million registered Palestine refugees in the Middle East."[19] It also employs terrorists.

In a sworn statement, Professor Rashid Khalidi of the University of Chicago testified that:

> Humanitarian and charitable institutions throughout Palestine employ personnel regardless of sectarian or political affiliation and offer services on a similar basis. Thus, UNRWA, NGO-run and public hospitals and clinics, for example, employ members of different political groups such as Fatah, the PFLP [Popular Front for the Liberation of Palestine], Hamas and Islamic Jihad, without reference to their belonging to a specific group.[20]

But al-Fatah, the PFLP, Hamas, and Islamic Jihad aren't merely political groups, the Palestinian equivalents of the Sierra Club or the Ripon Society. They are terrorist groups.

One of UNRWA's principal duties is to report terrorist activities it encounters. It utterly fails in that duty and—worse still—it appears to abet the terrorists' activities. On November 3, 2003, Israel's deputy UN ambassador, Arye Merkel, addressed the General Assembly to condemn UNRWA for its support of terrorism, pointing out that:

- In November 2002, Palestinian terrorists repeatedly fired on an Israeli military position in Gaza from the grounds of a UNRWA school while schoolchildren were there.

- In February 2003, Sama Bani Oudeh, an arrested Hamas operative, admitted that he had concealed explosives at a UNRWA school.
- Another Hamas operative, Nidal Abd el Fatah Abdullah Nazal, who worked as a UNRWA ambulance driver, admitted that he used the ambulance to ferry arms to terrorists and to pass operational orders among Hamas terrorists.
- Nahed Rashid Ahmed Attallah, a senior UNRWA employee in Gaza responsible for the distribution of assistance to refugees, admitted that he was an operative of both the PFLP and al-Fatah. He also admitted that he had used his UNRWA vehicle to help transport terrorists to attack Israeli soldiers and civilians. Nahed also used the vehicle to transport explosives to his brother-in-law Amer Karmout, an operative of the Palestinian Popular Resistance terrorist group.[21]

Because UNRWA does nothing to stop the terrorists, and because the Israelis do not search UN vehicles, UNRWA effectively helps the terrorists do their bloody work.

In my interview with Ziad abu Ziad, I asked him where the Palestinian Authority gets its funding, and he declined to answer. Later, I asked Ambassador Ayalon how much money is sent into the territories, and where it goes. Ayalon told me, "Since Arafat came to the Palestinian territories, they have received more than $5 billion in international aid. Per capita, that is more than the Europeans received after World War II," under the Marshall Plan.

So where does the money go? No one really knows, but, as Ambassador Ayalon pointed out, Arafat's personal wealth ranks him as the sixth wealthiest despot in the world.

The fact is that if the money being poured into the Palestinian areas were used for the benefit of the Palestinian people—instead of to support terror and to fill the pockets of Palestinian leaders—the West Bank and Gaza would look like Beverly Hills, not the ancient bullet-scarred shantytowns they now are. And the United Nations does nothing to hold Arafat accountable.

The UN preaches loudly that every state should fight against terrorism, but what does it do? It routinely cooperates with terrorists. The High Commission for Refugees, for example, lists dozens of NGO "donors and partners." According to a previously undisclosed CIA report drafted in 1998, some of these NGOs are known to be connected to terrorist organizations.

According to the CIA report:

> [N]early one-third of the Islamic NGOs in the Balkans have facilitated the activities of Islamic groups that engage in terrorism, including the Egyptian Al-Gama 'at al-Islamiyya, Palestinian Hamas, Algerian groups, and Lebanese Hizballah. Some of the terrorist groups such as al-Gama at al'Islamiyya have access to credentials for the UN High Commission for Refugees and other UN staffs in the former Yugoslavia.[22]

The CIA report mentions two High Commission "donors and partners" of particular interest: Human Appeal International, which has engaged in fund-raising for Hamas, and the Islamic Relief Agency, which ran guns in Bosnia, and, according to the CIA report, was controlled by Sudan's National Islamic Front.

What legitimacy does the UN have in the War on Terror? None.

CHAPTER THREE

"KOFIGATE":
THE UN OIL-FOR-FOOD PROGRAM

*"Never has there been a financial rip-off of the magnitude
of the UN oil-for-food scandal."*

—Syndicated columnist William Safire

THERE IS MORE THAN ENOUGH EVIDENCE TO CONCLUDE THAT THE UN Oil-for-Food program—and the UN officials who ran it—provided Saddam Hussein with the means to bribe politicians, to deprive his people of needed food and medicine, and to literally steal billions of dollars. There is even emerging evidence that money from the program might have gone to support al-Qaeda.[1] Compared to the UN, Enron and WorldCom are models of corporate probity.

The Oil-for-Food program was created in 1995 by Security Council Resolution 986 to "provide for the humanitarian needs of the Iraqi people," while Iraq was otherwise embargoed, until it fulfilled Security Council resolutions requiring its disarmament.[2] To achieve this humanitarian goal, the Security Council allowed "the import of petroleum and petroleum products originating in Iraq, including financial and other essential transactions directly relating thereto, sufficient to produce a sum not exceeding a total of one billion United States dollars every ninety days."[3]

The resolution required "transparency" for each transaction, which meant that Iraq's oil exports, the buyers' oil imports, and their financial transactions would be under UN supervision and documentation for later audit. Payments were to be made into a special escrow account established by Kofi Annan.

The UN's share of the money was to be limited to covering the expenses of the program itself, the expenses of the UN weapons inspectors, and paying for the food and humanitarian aid that would be distributed to the Iraqi people.[4] To cover these costs, the UN was allowed to take a fee of 2.2 percent of the oil sales. But evidence shows that the UN might have taken, and allowed Saddam to take, much more. The UN was acting as a fiduciary for the Iraqi people, holding that money in trust for them. That trust was violated in ways that if the UN program managers had been officers of a U.S. corporation, they would be on their way to jail.

The Oil-for-Food program was the biggest financial program ever handled by the UN. And it was the most corrupt—at least so far. In the eight years of its existence, the UN claims the Oil-for-Food program resulted in the export of 3.4 billion barrels of oil, with 72 percent of the revenue allegedly going to humanitarian needs.[5] But much of the oil revenues apparently went to line the pockets of UN officials— possibly including Kofi Annan—and politicians around the world. The way the program was run demonstrates the depth of the scandal, and the urgent need for an investigation in which the UN isn't left to investigate itself.

On March 8, 2004, Michael Soussan, a former Oil-for-Food program coordinator for the UN, wrote in the *Wall Street Journal*:

> Were UN employees supposed to oppose Security Council resolutions, lobby for a lifting of sanctions and whitewash

the regime? That is what a majority of our Baghdad staff did. No one took action to redress their behavior.

The small minority who sought to hold the regime accountable were overruled, sidelined and sometimes branded spies by our own leadership. Meanwhile, the Saddam regime had infiltrated our mission in Iraq. All of the 4,233 local staff hired by the UN were required to report to Iraqi intelligence services. At our Baghdad HQ, UN mission leaders saw no problem with assigning Iraqi staff to man our switchboard, fax machines and photocopy room. Our 151 international observers were under siege, spied on by their employees and sometimes threatened by Iraqi officials when they tried to communicate information to New York that was embarrassing to the regime. All of this severely curtailed the UN's ability to do its job.[6]

The UN, in other words, allowed its operation to be infiltrated and used by Iraqi intelligence. Worse, the food and medical supplies the Iraqis bought with UN money were sold at inflated prices so Saddam Hussein could pocket the margin. Often the food and medicine was unfit for use. As Soussan reported:

> [A]ccording to Security Council resolutions, the UN had a legal responsibility to report on any issue affecting the "adequacy, equitability and effectiveness" of the Oil-for-Food Program. Saddam's kickbacks affected all three aspects. There were many instances in the time I was there when the UN preferred to look the other way rather than address obvious signs of what was going wrong.
>
> Take the medical sector. The regime's decision to use kickback-friendly front companies to purchase drugs meant that hospitals often received medicines that were nearly expired or otherwise damaged from unscrupulous suppliers. Iraqi

doctors would complain about the quality of the drug supply to our UN observers. Kurdish leaders raised similar concerns directly with high-level UN officials. We knew exactly
how much the Iraqi government paid for any contract, and
we had the authority to inspect each shipment when it
crossed into Iraq. We had all the elements necessary to piece
together a clear picture of what was going on and alert the
Security Council to the fact that Saddam and his cronies
were buying poor quality products at inflated prices and
cashing in the difference. While the UN likes to claim this
was the most audited program in its history, I never once
read an audit report that raised questions about these practices—even though they were an open secret to anyone
involved in the program.[7]

The Iraqi Governing Council, which is building the new democratic
Iraq, has hired the Roland Berger Strategy Consultants firm to advise
it about, among other things, the Oil-for-Food program. After an initial investigation, Claude Hankes-Drielsma, chairman of UK operations
for Roland Berger, saw immediately that the Oil-for-Food program was
riddled with corruption.

In an urgent letter to UN secretary-general Kofi Annan dated
December 5, 2003, Hankes-Drielsma asked for an independent review
of the program:

As a result of my findings here, combined with earlier information, I most strongly urge the UN to consider appointing
an independent commission to review and investigate the
'Oil-for-Food Programme.'. . . My belief is that serious transgressions have taken place and may still be taking place.
    A further issue which needs most serious consideration
and on which I would welcome an early discussion with you
is how any debt which might have been incurred by Iraq

post–UN sanctions or made to rogue nations should be treated.

I spoke to Hankes-Drielsma on February 18, 2004. He had received no answer from Annan. But he had written another letter, this time to Hans Corell, the UN undersecretary for legal affairs and legal counsel. In that letter, Hankes-Drielsma specified the terms of the urgently needed investigation:

1. Oil-for-Food Program:
a. Indications are that not less than 10% was added to the value of all invoices to provide cash to Saddam Hussein (as much as $4 billion). If so, why was this not identified and prevented? Was the UN alerted to this at any stage? What action was taken and who was made aware of this allegation?
b. The UN received a fee of 2% of the value of all transactions to administer the program (as much as $1.1 billion US dollars.) What method was put in place by the UN to insure inspection of the quality of the food?
c. What controls were in place to monitor BNP [the bank of France] who handled the bulk of the [letters of credit], the total value of which may have [been] in the region of $47 billion US dollars?
d. The role of Jordanian Banks such as Jordan National Bank, Arab Bank and Housing Bank: Have there been a proper independent audit of all transactions and a proper accounting of all funds? Are these banks still holding funds, if so how much, why and how is this monitored? Was there a link between these banks and the Iraq Secret Service or any other part of the Saddam Hussein system?
e. Who at the UN carried overall responsibility for the Oil-for-Food program? Could there have been any link, directly or indirectly, with Saddam Hussein or middle men?

2. UN approval of Oil contracts under the [oil for food] program

a. Why did the UN approve oil contracts to non-end users? And without knowing the price?

b. A list of some of these contracts has been published by an Arab News Paper (this list which is known to me). It demonstrates beyond any doubt that Saddam Hussein bought political and other support under the aegis of the UN. In this list a "Mr. Sevan" is shown as receiving crude oil by this method through Panama.

c. VERY SIGNIFICANT SUPPLIES OF CRUDE OIL MADE TO NON-END USERS WERE TO OR TO THOSE LINKED TO INDIVIDUALS WITH POLITICAL INFLUENCE IN MANY COUNTRIES INCLUDING FRANCE AND JORDAN. WHAT METHOD OF CONTROL AND TRANSPARENCY OVER THESE SALES DID THE UN REQUIRE? [emphasis in original]

As of February 18, 2004, the UN was stonewalling. It issued a statement that said, in part:

It is thus entirely possible, indeed probable, that Saddam Hussein's regime used loopholes in the Security Council's resolutions and operating framework for the Oil-for-Food Program to extract illicit funds from both purchasers and suppliers. However, these funds did not pass through the UN. The program itself was managed strictly within the mandate given to it by the Security Council and was subject to nearly 100 different audits, external and internal, between 1998 and 2003 and, as the secretary-general has said, this produced no evidence of any wrongdoing by any UN official.[8]

The UN was trying to have it both ways. On one hand, it admitted that the Iraqi regime used the cover of the UN program to buy influence around the world, and possibly in the UN itself. On the other, the

UN demanded that the world simply take its word that the program was completely free of abuse and corruption, based on its own "audits." The UN was refusing access to its documentation and the individuals who ran the program.

But even with the UN stonewalling, Hankes-Drielsma was able to make some important findings. I asked him which countries had clearly traded illegally with Iraq when the UN sanctions prohibiting trade were in place. He was sure of only one: France. (He later told the press that Russia had also benefited from corruption in the Oil-for-Food program.)

One likely reason the UN wouldn't allow any open review of the Oil-for-Food program is that it would reveal that UN officials were on Saddam's payroll. The list Hankes-Drielsma referred to was published in January 2004 in the Iraqi newspaper *al-Mada*. The *al-Mada* list includes both people and nations who were receiving bribes from the Iraqi regime, in the form of oil allocations below market price, which could then be sold on the world market. Along with several nations—France and Russia among them—was the name Hankes-Drielsma referred to in his letter: "Mr. Sevan," listed under Panama, implying that there were payments into an account in that nation.[9] The head of the Oil-for-Food program since 1997 was Benon Sevan, UN assistant secretary-general.

Others on *al-Mada*'s long list of bribed individuals, entities, and countries, include:

- Russia, which, through various entities, received about 1.4 *billion* barrels of oil
- British politician George Galloway, a longtime pro-Saddam voice
- Indonesian president Megawati Sukarnoputri
- Canadian oil executive Arthur Millholland
- The foreign minister of Chad
- Eleven French individuals and companies

The evidence is growing that the UN Oil-for-Food program might have robbed tens of billions of dollars from the people of Iraq, and paid it to the friends of Saddam Hussein, who, in turn, agitated against America's policy of regime change in Iraq.

We don't know how many—or which—leading UN officials were bribed, because the UN will not reveal its financial accounts. In late March 2004, the UN tried to placate its critics with an internal investigation, but as Hankes-Drielsma told me, only an independent investigation can have any credibility. The Iraqi Governing Council agreed, hiring KPMG Peat Marwick, an American accounting firm, and Freshfields Bruckhaus Deringer, a British law firm, to investigate the program.

UN recalcitrance appeared to change on April 21, 2004, when Kofi Annan appointed an "independent" panel to investigate the Oil-for-Food scandal and the Security Council unanimously passed a new resolution "welcoming" it.[10] The panel is composed of Paul Volcker, former chairman of the U.S. Federal Reserve; Mark Pieth, a Swiss money laundering expert; and Richard Goldstone, a South African war crimes prosecutor; and all UN members were called upon to cooperate fully. But this investigation, which will use UN staff and offices, and won't have the power to compel cooperation from the citizens or banks of any nation, isn't likely to get to the bottom of the scandal.

Most of the money from the program passed through French banks, and several sources have told me that some of the money was siphoned off to bribe high-ranking French politicians, possibly including President Jacques Chirac. French banks handled nearly $50 billion in Oil-for-Food transactions, and anyone who believes the French—or the Russians, the Germans, the Jordanians, the Syrians, and the rest—will be forthcoming with documentation and witnesses essential to the investigation is dreaming. Thus, it will be impossible for the Annan-appointed investigators to uncover the evidence necessary to reveal the wrongdoing of the UN, or many of its culpable members and staff.

The UN is now setting itself up to loot Iraq again. Hankes-Drielsma told me that the new "Iraq Development Fund" the UN will administer will probably suffer from the same corruption as the Oil-for-Food program did. The United States and those few Security Council members interested in seeing Iraq rebuilt rather than looted by the UN have little time to ensure that the new fund is administered honestly—outside of UN control and auditing. The Volcker investigation is no proof that the UN can police itself, because it is hobbled by the lack of authority to subpoena witnesses or documents from people, businesses, and governments that decide not to cooperate. As always, the UN's credibility depends on the honesty of its members and staff. However, honesty is not a commodity in great supply at the UN.

CHAPTER FOUR

QUAGMIRE DIPLOMACY

"As a matter of common sense and self-defense,
America will act against such emerging [terrorist] threats
before they are fully formed. We cannot defend America
and our friends by hoping for the best."

—2002 National Security Strategy of the United States

FOR MORE THAN FIVE MONTHS, AMERICA DELAYED THE MILITARY OPER-
ations in Iraq while the UN debated. The insurgency in Iraq that is now
claiming lives of American and allied soldiers—and will do so for
months or years to come—was planned in those months. Not just in
Iraq, but in Iran, Syria, Egypt, and Saudi Arabia.

Beginning in November 2002 and continuing through mid-March
2003, the Iraqis hid weapons and money and organized cells of insurgents throughout their strongholds. More weapons were bought—some
from France and Russia—and smuggled in. Insurgents from other
nations—Jordanians, Syrians, Iranians, Sudanese and many others—
came in to fight against the freedom and democracy the United States
is trying to give Iraq. How many lives could have been spared had we
acted more quickly? Would we have caught Saddam with his weapons
of mass destruction (WMD) if we'd acted sooner?

In December 2002, Iraq reportedly began moving its WMD—its weapons, research and manufacturing equipment, records, and personnel—out of Iraq to Syria and Lebanon.[1] Right up to the beginning of the military campaign, people and materials were being moved into Syria on the highway from Baghdad through the border city of al-Qaim. After the Iraqi regime fell, the legitimacy of the war was called into question by Kofi Annan, French president Jacques Chirac, and many others who wanted to prove that the American action was illegal aggression because no WMD had been found.

America's *casus belli* was threefold: Iraq's WMD program, its connections to terrorism, and Saddam Hussein's oppression of the Iraqi people. But the principal justification for war was Saddam's WMD program, because it was a violation of the Gulf War cease-fire and UN resolution, as well as a serious threat to world peace. But now that American troops have failed to find WMD in Iraq, this justification has been, in the eyes of many, proven false. Though Saddam was hip-deep in terrorism, so are other nations in the Middle East and elsewhere. Why should America have singled out Iraq?

The better question is, why, if the president was convinced military action was essential, did he fail to go to war when the time was right?

While President George W. Bush readied the best-telegraphed military punch in American history, Saddam and his allies were acting. With regard to WMD, Deputy Secretary of Defense Paul Wolfowitz told me, "One possible area where they might have used that time is if they moved stuff to Syria, or buried stuff or otherwise hid stuff. We certainly know—I think [WMD search chief] David Kay has confirmed this—as Powell said in his February [2003] speech to the UN that they were...hiding things. And they were doing this most actively in the period after the resolutions....Evidence suggests that they were still cleaning things up after the war began, and even after the fall of Baghdad."

As soon as military action began, many of the top members of Saddam's regime fled to Syria, some used Syria as a transit point to other nations, and some even returned to Iraq. America underestimated the complicity and recklessness of the Syrian regime. Bashar Assad was convinced that America wouldn't attack Syria—and he was right.

I asked Paul Wolfowitz if Saddam gained military advantage because of the endless UN proceedings. He said, "I think relatively little. Because, maybe, Saddam never believed we would actually act. If that's the case—and I underline 'if that's the case' because we're really speculating here, wildly—one interpretation is that we may have some members of the Security Council to thank for that. And there is even a little bit of evidence of that point among the comments that have been made by some of the 'black list' people when they've been interviewed that suggests that they were convinced that the French would bail them out." (The "black list" people are those high in the Saddam regime who have been captured.)

Nevertheless, the cost of the UN delay is the time it gave Saddam and the terrorist neighbors of Iraq to plan the postwar insurgency and to move or hide WMD. At the beginning of 2004, President Bush was faced with a reelection campaign that was vastly more complicated by the apparent failure to find WMD stockpiles. More importantly, the failure to find WMD in Iraq hurt America's standing all over the world, but especially in the Arab countries, and gave critics an effective political weapon against America. Government-controlled media, such as Saudi Arabia's *Arab News*, are relentlessly critical of America generally and President Bush individually. The theory that Bush led America into an unnecessary war has become an accepted fact to the UN, to much of Europe, and, of course, to the Democratic Party of John Kerry.

The fact is that there is still no explanation of Iraq's WMD program, what form weapons might have been in (deployable weapons or merely research programs), or what had happened to them. The delay put on our military operation by the president's courting of the UN has hugely complicated the solving of that mystery.

Around 500 B.C., Chinese military philosopher Sun Tzu wrote that surprise and deception are two key principles of strategy.[2] In a war against terrorists and terrorist nations, surprise and deception are even more important. It was certain—even before Colin Powell's presentation to the General Assembly in February—that the UN would not act. But for yet another month, we stayed our hand while the UN kabuki dance played on.

In Afghanistan, America succeeded in destroying the Taliban regime and the terrorist infrastructure—training camps and safe havens—that enabled terrorists to mount large-scale attacks. In Iraq, American forces defeated the Iraqi army, but the other necessary level of success—capturing and destroying Iraq's WMD—required surprise. UN diplomacy and preemption cannot coexist. We have to choose one or the other. If the subordination of U.S. war plans to UN diplomacy is repeated, it will be fatal to George W. Bush's strategy of preempting terrorist attacks by military action.

The diplomatic delay to the Iraq War was costly in the most important sense: in blood. Intelligence sources said—all through the period of quagmire diplomacy—that terrorists from other nations were slipping into Iraq, and that Iraq was receiving military supplies from nations—France and Russia—that were supposedly supporting UN diplomacy. And the Iraqis were given time to plan an insurgency, in coordination with the terrorists.

That insurgency went into action almost as soon as the Saddam statue was toppled in Firdos Square in Baghdad, and continues. As of February 10, 2004, more than 530 Americans had died in Iraq, more than half of them after May 1, 2003, when the major military action in Iraq was declared over.[3] How many of these lives were lost because the Iraqis and the terrorists had been given time to plan their insurgency is unknowable, as is how many lives would have been spared had the diplomatic effort been shortened. But the point is the same: Subordinating military action to diplomacy in preemptive war cannot work.

Preemption of terrorist threats is essential to preventing future terrorist attacks such as those of September 11, 2001. Preemptive action does not have to be unilateral. Diplomacy—outside the UN, forging other "coalitions of the willing"—can precede military action. But it can be done only in secret, involving allies in military plans before attacks are carried out. That sort of diplomacy—linked closely to the decision to preempt, and integrated into military planning—can help avoid the principal failure of the Iraq campaign: the failure to prevent the terrorist nation from arranging for its most important assets to escape the preemptive strike. Deception is as much a part of diplomacy as secrecy and surprise are parts of war-making.

The damage of the UN-imposed delay will last for decades. If we do not find Saddam's WMD, America will be branded an unjustified aggressor that lied its way into war, and few nations—even our closest allies, such as Britain—will join us in another military campaign. Because the UN will not change, we cannot again step into its quagmire of diplomacy.

CHAPTER FIVE

SECRETARY-GENERAL KOFI ANNAN: A SYMPTOM OF THE UN DISEASE

"I admire the martial and commanding air with which the right honorable gentleman treats the facts. He stands no nonsense from them."

—Winston Churchill, speaking of a parliamentary foe

IN 1997, KOFI ANNAN OF GHANA BEGAN HIS FIRST TERM AS SECRETARY-general. These days, we are used to seeing Annan walking down lines of blue-bereted UN troops, reviewing them as though he were their commander in chief. It is by assumption of that role—completely unjustified by the UN Charter, but encouraged by France, Germany, Russia, and others, including America's Democratic Party—that the UN secretary-general has been transformed from an administrative officer into someone with the pretension and grandiosity of a head of state.

Kofi Annan is the most activist secretary-general—at least in a self-serving sense—the UN has ever had. Rather than encouraging members to deal with international crises, he has sought to expand the UN's prominence and influence for its own sake.

"So yeah, I'm still pretty much for the UN. I still think Kofi Annan's a good guy who deserved the Nobel Peace Prize." This was former president

Bill Clinton's assessment (in April 2003) of the man who—on Clinton's watch—became not only the pal of Saddam Hussein, but worked to thwart action against terrorists and the nations that support them.

Richard Butler was the head of the UN special commission (UNSCOM) charged with ensuring that Saddam had disarmed Iraq of WMD. He began his book about his years in UNSCOM by writing:

> The greatest threat to life on earth is weapons of mass destruction—nuclear, chemical, biological. These weapons do not exist in nature. They have been made by man, generally as the result of sophisticated research, and complex, costly processes.
>
> The community of nations has recognized this threat; indeed, perhaps the most important achievement in the second half of the twentieth century was the weaving of a tapestry of treaties designed to contain and then eliminate it. This work was never easy, and its implementation has been challenged repeatedly. The most determined and diabolical of such challenges has been mounted by the dictator of Iraq—Saddam Hussein.
>
> For almost two decades, he has sought to acquire these weapons and the means of their delivery. In most cases, he has been successful and even took the further step of using them.... He shares with Adolf Hitler the infamy of having used chemicals for genocidal purposes.[1]

Butler's job was tough enough, but Kofi Annan's personal interference made the job impossible.

UN Security Council Resolution 687 stated the terms of the cease-fire of the first Gulf War. It required that Saddam:

> Shall accept unconditionally the destruction, removal or rendering harmless, under international supervision, of: (a) all

chemical and biological weapons and all stocks of agents and related subsystems and components and all research, development, support and manufacturing facilities related thereto; and (b) all ballistic missiles with a range greater than one hundred and fifty kilometers, and all related major parts and repair and production facilities.[2]

Violation of the terms of the cease-fire, by any reading of international law, meant that a state of war again existed. But Kofi Annan didn't see it that way. For him, the cease-fire was forever negotiable, regardless of continued Iraqi violations.

By 1998, the UN Security Council had passed six resolutions requiring Saddam to disarm, and he had failed to comply with every one of them. American and British pilots, enforcing the "no-fly" zones, from which Iraqi aircraft were prohibited entry, faced almost daily ground fire and surface-to-air missile attack by the Iraqis. UNSCOM weapons inspectors were denied entry to the hundred or so "presidential sites" that were prime locations to discover WMD. Many of these sites—some of them ten or fifteen square miles in size and including almost one hundred buildings—were known to conceal extensive underground complexes. A cacophony of intelligence reports about WMD activities at these sites—some from Iraqi National Congress sources in Iraq—poured in.[3]

Saddam demanded "modalities"—written procedures regarding how inspections would be conducted—before allowing Butler's UNSCOM inspectors access to the presidential palaces and other sites. Those "modalities"—first established in 1996—hampered UNSCOM's ability to conduct no-notice inspections, and limited access to too many sites for the inspectors' job to be done properly.[4]

Annan sided with the Iraqis, thus tabling any hope of the inspections succeeding. Butler was forced to accept a Russian and a Frenchman on his staff, who of course acted as agents of their governments, which disapproved of intrusive UNSCOM inspections.[5]

The UN Charter, in uncharacteristically clear and strong language, requires that the staff of the secretary-general be independent of instruction from individual governments, and member governments agree to not seek to influence them.[6] This rule has never been followed. Ambassador Jose Sorzano, who served as Jeane Kirkpatrick's UN deputy during the Reagan administration, told me that the Soviet Union consistently broke the rule. Richard Butler also found this to be an "empty rule" while heading UNSCOM.[7] But Butler's biggest problem wasn't with the staff. It was with the secretary-general himself.

In February 1998, Annan flew to Baghdad. He went without instructions from the Security Council and without any authority to negotiate away the terms of the cease-fire resolution.[8] But that's exactly what he did.

In several meetings, at one of which he was photographed bowing to Saddam Hussein,[9] Annan made an agreement reinstituting the "modalities" Butler had fought so hard to eliminate, and agreed to other "special procedures" that fettered the inspections of Saddam's palaces.[10] After Annan sold out the inspectors, the Security Council ratified the Annan agreement, with the Clinton administration's approval. As Butler saw it, "I had no illusions about what had happened—UNSCOM's mandate had, at least in part, been bargained away in Baghdad."[11]

In the end, Saddam kicked UNSCOM out of Iraq in August 1998, declaring its work done. Once again, Annan and his staff—with the help of the French and the Russians—stepped in to advocate a "comprehensive review" of the Iraqi disarmament, which was completed two months later. The report concluded that Iraq had not complied with its obligations and that sanctions should stay in place. Saddam responded by rejecting any cooperation with UNSCOM, and demanded that Butler be removed as chairman.[12]

American and British military forces eventually compelled Saddam to agree to let UNSCOM inspectors resume their efforts on November 15, 1998. But once again, the Iraqis denied them access to crucial sites. So on December 16, 1998, American and British aircraft—as well as about two hundred cruise missiles—began hitting military targets in Iraq to force Saddam to comply.

Three days later, President Clinton addressed the nation, telling us that the "seventy-hour" strategy had worked and that Saddam's WMD programs had been degraded.[13] But in fact, though British and American jets had bombed almost one hundred targets, Saddam had not bound himself to any verifiable disarmament, and the Clinton administration had shown yet again that it was satisfied with spin rather than substance. As the victors of the Gulf War, the British and Americans had every right to enforce the cease-fire agreement requiring Iraq's disarmament independently of the United Nations. But the Clinton administration never took that decisive action.

Another UN inspection team was formed. It was called UNMOVIC: the UN Monitoring, Verification, and Inspection Commission. Its head, Hans Blix, was a Swedish diplomat who was far less aggressive than Richard Butler and became a vocal opponent of the war with Iraq.

On January 14, 2003, Annan was asked about a statement by British foreign minister Jack Straw that Britain reserved the right to act militarily against Iraq without Security Council approval. Annan disagreed. "I think the Council discussions and the Council resolutions, which guide me, make it quite clear that they will have to go to the Council for further discussions, and for the Council—which has threatened serious consequences—I hope, to also determine what those consequences would be."[14]

On March 13, 2003, Annan was asked whether U.S. military action against Iraq, without Security Council approval, violated the UN Charter. He answered, "If the U.S. and others were to go outside the Council and take military action, it would not be in conformity with the Charter."[15]

But if the Iraq campaign was a violation of the UN Charter, then so was the Afghanistan campaign, which was undertaken without UN permission, and so were France's military interventions in the Ivory

Coast and the Central African Republic in 2003. Moreover, if, by Kofi Annan's thinking, the U.S. was in violation of the UN Charter, it was also acting in violation of international law.

Annan and the UN General Assembly are silent about the most egregious violations of the UN Charter regarding terrorism. Syria and Iran, for example, are members in good standing. But Kofi Annan and the UN would like to create a legal shackle on United States foreign policy by means of the International Criminal Court.

Kofi's Court

The International Criminal Court (ICC) was created by the Rome Statute to have universal jurisdiction over war crimes and crimes against humanity.[16] Universal jurisdiction is something new—and dangerous. The ICC has expanded the definition of "war crimes" far beyond that established by the Geneva Convention. Among the new definitions are "environmental crimes" and attacks that might cause incidental loss of life.[17] Careful where you pitch that tent, soldier. Don't disturb that spotted owl nesting in the tree above you. And don't even think of bombing that building where your enemy has his headquarters. The enemy is smart enough to have set up camp with protected wetlands to one side and an endangered species to the other. The Rome Statute has even made it possible to prosecute as "war criminals" U.S. soldiers who take terrorists prisoner and isolate them—as at Guantanamo Bay, Cuba—for interrogation. Bill Clinton signed the treaty implementing the ICC on December 31, 2000, but did not submit it for Senate ratification. In other words, he tried, extra-legally, to bind the United States to the UN's latest power grab.

And a power grab it clearly was. Under one reading of the ICC law, not only soldiers and generals, but presidents and Cabinet ministers could be punished by the International Criminal Court for war crimes and for violating UN resolutions. As former secretary of state Henry Kissinger pointed out, in its current form the ICC represents a fundamental assault on American sovereignty, rights, and practices under the Constitution.[18]

Kissinger writes:

> Distrusting national governments, many of the advocates of universal jurisdiction seek to place politicians under the supervision of magistrates and the judicial system. But prosecutorial discretion without accountability is precisely one of the flaws of the International Criminal Court. Definitions of relevant crimes are vague and highly susceptible to politicized application. Defendants will not enjoy due process as understood in the United States. Any signatory state has the right to trigger an investigation. As the US experience with special prosecutors investigating the executive branch shows, such a procedure is likely to develop its own momentum without time limits and can turn into an instrument of political warfare.[19]

President George W. Bush has rightly rejected the ICC treaty, and took the trouble to negotiate immunity for U.S. forces serving as UN peacekeepers, ensuring that the ICC could not prosecute them. Kofi Annan opposed him, and in June 2003, addressed the Security Council before it voted on whether to extend—by one year—that immunity. Annan said approving immunity from ICC prosecution would undermine the "legitimacy" of peacekeeping. He criticized the United States for giving the impression that "it wished to claim an absolute and permanent immunity for people serving in the operations [the Security Council] establishes."[20] Annan lobbied hard against America's position, and lost. The fight will recur as long as the ICC is in existence, or until America ceases to participate in UN peacekeeping missions.

The ICC is finding other ways to expand its power. One of these is broadening the Geneva Convention's limited definition of prohibited weapons. Under the Convention, poison gas and biological warfare are outlawed. Cluster bombs—which dispense hundreds of small bombs over a target area—are highly effective against concentrations of troops, and some have the capability to destroy armored vehicles as well.[21] At this writing, seven academics are bringing a case against British use of cluster bombs in the 2003 Iraq campaign, and the ICC has launched an investigation that might result in war crime indictments against British commanders, even against Prime Minister Tony Blair.[22] Included in the investigation is the use of bunker-busting bombs that penetrate and destroy underground targets. A group calling itself "Peacerights" wants to have the ICC declare the Iraq campaign itself illegal. One of its lawyers, Professor Bill Bowring of London Metropolitan University, said, "The U.S. cannot be tried before the court because it refuses to sign up to [the ICC treaty]. The UK did."[23] Just so.

Meanwhile, George W. Bush has repeatedly invited the UN to help rebuild Iraq, but Kofi Annan has resisted cooperation with the United States, because the UN would not have full control of the effort. "I need to weigh the degree of risk that the UN is being asked to accept against the substance of the role we are being asked to fulfill," he said.[24]

Annan misses no chance to assert the UN's power. When Saddam Hussein was captured on December 13, 2003, Annan promptly declared that Hussein should not be sentenced to the death penalty in any trial. "The UN does not support the death penalty," he said. "In all the courts we have set up [UN officials] have not included death penalty."[25] That a sovereign government of Iraq might execute Saddam in accordance with its own laws is irrelevant to the secretary-general. To him, only the UN should rule.

The Legitimacy Scam

"Colin in Kofi Land" was the headline of a *Wall Street Journal* editorial on October 13, 2003, which made two very important points. First:

> The apparent failure of the U.S. push for another UN resolution on Iraq is at least a clarifying moment. A body incapable of agreeing to endorse even post facto reconstruction could certainly never have been expected to enforce its Iraq resolutions in the first place. So much for the argument that

a kinder, gentler approach by the Bush administration would have won UN support.[26]

That proposed resolution, which didn't give the French and Germans the control of post-Saddam Iraq they demanded, proved redundantly that the Security Council had ceased to perform its principal duty: to deal with threats to peace. But the second point was even more important:

> UN Secretary General Kofi Annan has made it clear that he's now more interested in defeating President Bush than he ever was in toppling Saddam Hussein. Mr. Annan knows that Mr. Bush's policy...poses a serious challenge to what he claims is the "unique legitimacy" of the collection of despots he leads—indeed to the legitimacy of the unaccountable Secretary General himself.[27]

Annan realizes that any time the United States acts without first getting permission of the UN Security Council, it reduces the power and influence of the UN, and thus his own power and influence. In setting the agenda for his "reform" panel, Annan planned to deal thusly with the American threat to UN power:

> I have tried to work with the Members to find ways of improving our Organization to make it more effective, and in fact also of trying to develop international law, because some of the questions that the panel will have to deal with touch on not just structures and process of the United Nations, but how the international community organizes to cooperate and organizes itself to ensure that we maintain peace and security. And it really is pushing the development of international law where they will have to discuss questions of when preventive war is acceptable, under what rules and who approves.[28]

"Under what rules, and who approves." That's the only issue in Annan's mind, and in the minds of the UN's most faithful supporters. Annan is more interested in increasing the UN's power to control American action than he is in doing the job for which he was hired. Kofi Annan and Jacques Chirac see the UN—as do too many others, including the leaders of the Democratic Party—as a brake on America's drive to preempt the terrorist threats it faces. Who approves preemptive action, the UN or the United States acting as a sovereign nation in accordance with our Constitution? That's the only issue for the UN's supporters, for the American people, and for our president.

The legitimacy of Annan's actions—of every UN action—derives from UN member states' legitimacy. International consensus can grant legitimacy, but only if that consensus comes from free nations. The Warsaw Pact always had a consensus among its members, because those "members" had no choice. In treaties, nations make binding agreements that carry the legitimacy of international law. Whether Annan sprinkles UN holy water over something doesn't make it bad or good. Legitimacy in international affairs results from nations acting peacefully, in their political and economic interests, or militarily, to resist aggression and repel or preempt an attack. Facts give rise to legitimacy. The UN, as much as it might like to, cannot create or destroy such facts.

CHAPTER SIX

THE UN BUREAUCRACY: NICE WORK IF YOU CAN GET IT

"Even though most staff join the UN out of support for the ideals of the Organization, the UN still has difficulty in attracting and retaining staff from countries with high pay levels. If the UN wants to continue to attract highly qualified and dedicated professionals, it must be a competitive employer offering attractive conditions."

—UN website

AMERICAN TAXPAYERS SPEND MORE ON THE UN THAN THEY KNOW, because while most people look at our UN dues, that's only about half the bill. The other half is made up of voluntary contributions and subsidiary dues. All told, in 2004 America will throw about $7 billion down the UN drain.

Ever since the UN was founded, the U.S. has been its biggest source of funds. Under the UN's scale of assessments, the United States now pays a maximum of 22 percent of the entire UN's "regular" budget, while some forty-six nations are asked to pay only the minimum—0.001 percent[1]—and some fail to pay altogether. In 2003, the assessed dues for the regular UN—not counting the other dues and voluntary contributions—amounted to almost $3.5 billion.[2] Some large nations, Russia and China, for example, were assessed only $18.6 million and $23.7 million respectively in 2003.[3]

Not included in the basic UN assessment are the "voluntary" contributions America makes to a large number of UN programs.

 Looking at the UN's mass of programs and activities—and its huge,
overpaid bureaucracy—it's easy to see how the UN burns up all that
money so quickly. What is not so easy to understand is why the bud-
getary reforms insisted on by the United States and other nations are
not happening, except that Congress is so easily fooled by the UN.

For example, according to a 2003 study by the Congressional
Research Service (CRS), reforms imposed by Kofi Annan are reducing
the size of the UN bureaucracy.[4] Unfortunately, the CRS study is flat-
out wrong.

In 1947, when Trygve Lie was the first secretary-general, the UN
staff was about 1,200 strong.[5] According to the CRS report, Annan's
"reforms" have cut the UN Secretariat's staff—which serves not just
the office of the secretary-general but the myriad UN agencies around
the world—from about twelve thousand employees to fewer than nine
thousand today.[6] But, as the *Wall Street Journal* points out, "The staff
of the Secretariat, the central bureaucracy that serves core UN agencies, is a patchwork of entrenched employees with permanent contracts
and others with little job security." According to the UN's own website, and the *Journal*'s analysis of its data, the UN Secretariat staff
hasn't been cut to nine thousand: It has grown to more than seventeen
thousand. So much for Annan's reforms.

The increase has been concealed—at least from the supposedly prob-
ing eye of the Congressional Research Service—by shifting employees
from permanent to non-permanent status. By increasing the numbers
of non-permanent employees—employees whose job security now
depends on the secretary-general's favor—Annan has created a bureaucracy to serve his own agenda.

By UN rule, staff salaries are among the highest in the world. The
salaries are set in accordance with the "Noblemaire Principle," which,
according to the UN, states that "the international civil service should be
able to recruit staff from its Member states, including the highest-paid."[7]

Consider the salaries of many of those seventeen thousand UN bureaucrats:

- Thirty-six undersecretaries-general, each drawing a salary of $186,144, plus home leave and family visit travel expenses, rent subsidies, U.S. tax exemptions, expense accounts for entertainment, and various other perks
- Forty assistant secretaries-general, paid $169,366, plus similar perks
- 433 directors, paid between $126,713 and $154,223, plus perks
- 5,106 professionals, paid between $42,944 and $131,299 (yes, plus perks)
- 6,795 "general services" employees, paid between $30,147 and $80,232[8]

That adds up to about seventeen thousand UN bureaucrats pulling down a total of just shy of $1 billion. Nice work if you can get it. And you can, if you play the game.

ET Went Home, UN Bureaucrats Don't

There are 191 member nations of the UN General Assembly, and the vast majority of them are impoverished, bereft of every political and economic freedom Americans enjoy.[9] When their staff land in New York, they live in a free and luxurious world unlike anything they have ever experienced—or could experience—at home. They like it, and they want to stay. And because they want to stay, they work their way into the UN bureaucracy.

Slowly, over the years, bureaucrats from the Third World have taken over the UN staff. In 1946, only 20 percent of the UN Secretariat's staff was from Central and South America, Africa, the Middle East, and Central, East, and Southeast Asia. The remaining 80 percent were from North America and Europe.[10] During the Cold

Table 3. U.S. Voluntary Contributions
the Foreign Assistance Act (International Organ

	FY2001 Actual
UN Development Program (UNDP)	87
UN Children's Fund (UNICEF)[b]	109
World Food Program (WFP)	5
UN Development Fund for Women (UNIFEM)	1
International Contributions for Scientific, Educational, & Cultural Activities	1.8
WMO Voluntary Co-op Program	2
UN Environment Program (UNEP)	10
Montreal Protocol Multilateral Fund	26
International Conservation Programs[c] (CITES, ITTO, IUCN, Ramsar, CCD)	5.5
UN Voluntary Fund Torture Victims	5
Climate Stabilization Fund (IPCC, UNFCC)	6.5
ICAO Aviation Security Fund	.3
UN Voluntary Fund for Advisory Services & Technical Cooperation	1.5
IAEA Voluntary Programs[d]	50.5
UN Guards in Iraq	—
UN Population Fund (UNFPA)[e]	21.5
Reserved—To Be Allocated	—
Total	**333.6**

a) Does not include U.S. contributions to UN High Commissioner for Refugee (UNHCR) programs ($255 million in FY2002) and to UN Relief and Works Agency for Palestine Refugees in the Near East (UNRWA) ($119 million in FY2002), financed through the Migration and Refugee Assistance Account; World Food Program commodities donations; WHO Special Programs; UN Volunteers; and UN International Drug Control Program.
b) Appropriated under Child Survival Program.

to UN Programs Financed Through
izations and Programs) a(in millions of dollars)

FY2002 Actual	FY2003 Estimate	FY2004 Request
97	100	100
120	120	120
6	—	6
1	1	1
1.8	1.8	.5
2	2	2
10.8	10	10
25	23	21
7.7	6.2	6.2
5	5	5
7.4	5.6	5.6
.3	.3	1
1.5	1.5	1.5
49	50	50
—	—	.7
—	—	—
—	25	25
335.5	**351.4**	**355.5**

c) Only CITES is a UN program.

d) Requested and Appropriated under Non-Proliferation, Antiterrorism, Demining and Related Programs account.

e) Congress appropriated $34 million for FY2002, but the State Department determined that UNFPA was ineligible for the U.S. contribution. $34 million was appropriated for FY2003 provided that eligibility can be certified.

War, there was a pronounced shift in favor of Communist states. Former UN ambassador Jeane Kirkpatrick told me, "The Secretariat was then [in the 1980s] heavily infiltrated with Soviet personnel who were engaged in espionage activity. The Soviets and Cubans were both grossly overrepresented inside the Secretariat. That's changed now." By 2003, the problem wasn't Communist subversion, but Third World domination.

According to the *Wall Street Journal*'s summary of UN data on its staff, in 2003:

- 12 percent were from Central and South America
- 19 percent were from Africa
- 5 percent were from the Middle East or Central Asia
- 18 percent were from East and Southeast Asia

In sum, North American and Europe—the democratic West—is now in the minority, and more than half of the UN Secretariat's employees come from the Third World.[11] While the U.S. provides most of the money for the UN, the Third World provides most of the people who determine and implement the UN agenda.

"The Name of the Game Is the Game"

That's what former U.S. economic counselor Dennis Goodman said about the culture of the UN. Goodman, a career foreign service officer, spent six years butting his head against the UN bureaucracy. "They don't care whether they're talking about commodity prices or transnational corporations," he told me. Every resolution from ECOSOC—the UN's Economic and Social Council, for which he worked—had to end with the magic words: "The secretary-general should study this resolution and report back to ECOSOC," thus ensuring another round of meetings and more study. And longer job security for the bureaucrats. In essence, the UN has become an American-subsidized program to employ Third World bureaucrats. "They think the U.S. treasury is the common heritage of mankind," said Goodman. To that end, Third World countries sign treaties that cost them nothing, but can cost developed nations dearly. The Lebanese, for example, have signed on to all sorts of UN-generated treaties, such as Biodiversity, Climate Change, Desertification, Hazardous Wastes, Law of the Sea, Nuclear Test Ban, Ozone Layer Protection, Ship Pollution, and Wetlands.[12] All of these treaties put burdens on our economy, not Lebanon's.

Here's how America's taxpayer billions, in fiscal year 2004, will be spent at the UN:

United Nations	$340.7 (in millions)
UN War Crimes Tribunal	$30
Iraq War Crimes Commission	$2
Food and Agriculture Organization	$72.4
International Atomic Energy Agency	$54.3
International Civil Aviation Agency	$12.6
International Labor Organization	$50.4
International Maritime Organization	$1.2
International Telecommunications Union	$6.6
UN Educational, Scientific, and Cultural Organization	$71.5
Universal Postal Union	$1.3
World Health Organization	$93.6
World Intellectual Property Organization	$1
World Meteorological Organization	$8.3
TOTAL:	**$746 million**[13]

In truth, some of these agencies do the Lord's work. Do we want to immunize millions in Africa against smallpox? We did, and the World Health Organization did it. Some humanitarian UN agencies work well, but many do not.

One of the best examples is the UN Human Rights Commission (HRC), which the United States helped create in 1947. In May 2001, the U.S. was thrown off the Commission while Sudan—one of the few nations that allows slavery and is one of the worst abusers of human rights on the planet—was voted on. Libya was elected chair of the committee. Today, the HRC is composed of fifty-three members, including Communist China, Cuba, Sudan, Nigeria, Saudi Arabia, and Zimbabwe, among the most severe abusers of human rights in the world. And yet the United States has rejoined the HRC's membership, lending its good name to this farce. Why? Because it's the UN, that's why.

By participating in such UN forums, we contribute to the UN's spread of corruption and propaganda. If talk is cheap in America, it's altogether free at the UN. The UN document system enables every delegation to have its scribblings circulated as "official" UN documents.[14] Jose Sorzano, Jeane Kirkpatrick's deputy UN ambassador, wrote, "In this manner all sorts of propaganda are later distributed with the UN's imprimatur."[15] The UN corrupts debate by giving propaganda a dignity it could never otherwise have.

And what is our reward for consenting to this corruption? More bills, and an endless stream of proposed treaties, resolutions, and other claptrap designed to burden our economy and raid our treasury. At the end of 2002, the UN said we still owed it $12 million for "international tribunals" (not including the International Criminal Court), $535 million for peacekeeping missions (which is over and above the congressionally set cap of 25 percent of the entire UN peacekeeping budget), and $190 million in back dues.[16]

On November 22, 1999, Senator John Kerry wrote in the *Washington Times*, "When we fail to pay our U.N. dues, we undermine support from our friends and allies who stand by us in places such as Kosovo and Iraq." But the support of friends and allies can't be bought at the UN. It can be gained only by sharing values and goals. All too few of the UN's members share any of America's values, goals, or interest in preserving freedom.

CHAPTER SEVEN

THE UN'S FATAL FLAWS

"Far along the world-wide whisper of the south-wind rushing warm,
With the standards of the peoples plunging thro' the thunder-storm;
Till the war-drum throbb'd no longer, and the battle flags were furl'd
In the Parliament of man, the Federation of the world.
There the common sense of most shall hold a fretful realm in awe,
And the kindly earth shall slumber, lapt in universal law."

—Alfred, Lord Tennyson, "Locksley Hall"

IN THE ATLANTIC CHARTER OF JULY 1941, FRANKLIN DELANO ROOSEVELT and Winston Churchill framed, in rather wishful terms, their vision of a postwar world of peaceful, self-governing nations participating in "a wider and permanent system of general security," including disarmament.[1] In February 1942, representatives of twenty-six nations met in Washington and signed a "United Nations" declaration, pledging to fulfill the Atlantic Charter.[2] By the spring of 1943, the United States had a fairly complete draft of a UN charter, which had been shared with the British.[3]

In February 1945, months before Germany or Japan surrendered, the leaders of the major powers—America, Britain, and Russia—gathered at the Black Sea resort of Yalta to discuss the postwar world and outlined what would become the UN. From the start, pretending that Joseph

Stalin shared the goals of the Atlantic Charter was a farce. But there was another weasel in the woodpile: Charles de Gaulle, the very model of the modern pestilential Frenchman, whose pomposity earned the dislike of both Roosevelt and Churchill. At the Casablanca Conference in 1942, the British prime minister and American president met with de Gaulle.

> Brendan Bracken, who was in charge of Churchill's arrangements at the hectic three-day meetings, at one point vented his frustrations at his boss. Churchill replied, "Well, Brendan, you have only one cross to bear. I have a double cross—the double cross of Lorraine."
> "The general's problem," sympathized Bracken, "is that he thinks he is the reincarnation of Joan of Arc."
> "No, the problem is," concluded Churchill, "my bishops won't allow me to burn him."[4]

Roosevelt's dislike for de Gaulle, less eloquently expressed than Churchill's, nevertheless had a greater effect. Roosevelt excluded de Gaulle from the 1944 Dumbarton Oaks conference, at which the UN charter was further developed, and again from the Yalta summit at which the postwar world took shape. Because de Gaulle wasn't included in the summit, he reached a state of indignation that only the French can achieve, and which—as the president of the Free French nation—he shared with the rest of the Free French government.

The exclusion of France wasn't the result of a petty personality conflict. By no measure could post–World War II France be considered one of the world's great powers. Its crushed economy would take many years to recover. It had no significant army, air force, or navy. In short, France demanded recognition as a world power despite the fact that it clearly wasn't one.

Having been excluded from Yalta, de Gaulle at first turned down a permanent seat on the UN Security Council and said he would not send a French delegation to the final drafting conference in San Francisco.

But, as the conference grew near, de Gaulle changed his mind and agreed that France would be a sponsor of the conference.[5] To soothe de Gaulle's bruised ego, American secretary of state Edward Stettinius asked him to reconsider his rejection of the permanent Security Council seat, and de Gaulle consented.

By the time the San Francisco conference began in late April 1945, Roosevelt was dead and Harry Truman, who had been involved in the UN preparations since 1943,[6] was president. Truman was even more of a dreamer than Roosevelt had been. He had a favorite poem that had he recited from a very young age: Alfred, Lord Tennyson's "Locksley Hall."[7] The poem envisions a "parliament of man" ruling over a peaceful, untroubled world—something, unfortunately, that the UN would never be.

One of the greatest bones of contention in the San Francisco conference was the authority of the Security Council. Under the proposed UN charter, the General Assembly could do what it liked; no nation was bound by General Assembly resolutions. The Security Council was another matter. To overcome the perceived weakness of the former League of Nations, the new UN Security Council's resolutions were supposed to be binding on all member states.

The Soviets had been expelled from the League of Nations because of their attack on Finland in the early days of World War II. To ensure that Soviet Russia wasn't expelled from the UN, Stalin demanded a veto over Security Council resolutions, and he got it. When the San Francisco conference ended, the Security Council was structured with five permanent members and six non-permanent members that would be elected to two-year terms.[8] All five permanent members were given the veto. And, of course, one of the permanent members was France. Blame the State Department, blame the Russians, blame whomever you'd like, the result is the same: France and Soviet Russia held veto power over every crucial UN decision.

There are many defects in the UN Charter. Some of them made the failure of the organization inevitable:

- False equality among nations: Article 2 says, "The Organization is based on the principle of sovereign equality of all its Members." Equality among men—the foundational principle of democracy—is false when applied to nations. Men are created equal, but nations are not. There might be nothing wrong with democracy among the well intentioned, but when the membership of a global body includes dictatorships, terrorists, and Communists, there must be a means of distinguishing between those members who are willing to respect human rights and neighbors' borders and those who aren't.

- Membership: Any nation, pseudo-nation, or thugocracy, such as Iran under the mullahs, can be a member of the UN. Under Article 4, if the Security Council recommends admission and the General Assembly approves the recommendation, the nation becomes a member. Unless the Security Council recommends it, no nation can have its UN membership suspended or taken away.[9] In practical terms, that doesn't work. When a legitimate government is overthrown by a totalitarian one, the totalitarians take the UN seat. Because Britain and the United States refused to support it in the Security Council, populous and economically successful Taiwan, one of the few real democracies in the Pacific, and a traditional ally of the United States, was expelled from the UN and replaced by Communist China.

- Accountability: Although the secretary-general is the chief administrative officer of the UN, the Charter creates no system of checks and balances on UN operations. The opportunity for corruption—illustrated by the Oil-for-Food program—is enormous.

But structural defects aside, the UN's failure has been shown by experience.

Does the UN Work?

It's fair to ask: Just what does the UN do? It's far easier to say what it doesn't do. It hasn't created a world at peace and, to be fair, nothing can. General Douglas MacArthur, in his famous 1962 farewell at West Point, quoted Plato: "Only the dead have seen an end to war."[10] But the UN fails in most of its appointed tasks, even the ones in which it could find success.

Many UN adherents still claim that the organization works. And— to be perfectly Clintonesque—we need to agree on what "work" means. For the UN to work, we shouldn't expect it to be merely an instrument of American policy. Rather, it must be a serious forum for debate and decision. In fact, according to its Charter, it was supposed to be precisely what President Bush asked it to be in 2002: a means for coalitions of nations to form, and thus to oppose—diplomatically at first, and militarily if necessary—aggression against any member nation.[11] The endless debates and the dealings with Saddam Hussein's Iraq prove that the UN failed in that task. As an agent of global coalescence to oppose and defeat terrorism, the UN has rendered itself useless. It is broken in almost every material aspect.

In short:

- The General Assembly is broken because its principal purpose has been shoved aside in favor of political polemics designed to degrade the influence of the United States and its allies.

- The Security Council is broken because the alliances upon which it was founded no longer exist, and the interests of the powers that have a veto over Security Council resolutions have diverged to a point that consensus and action cannot be achieved.

- The secretary-general's office is broken because the incumbent is more interested in increasing the authority of the UN than he is in aiding its members in fighting terrorism or real

threats to peace. Supporting him in this, the bureaucracy of
the Secretariat is dedicated to a Third World agenda that
mirrors the dysfunctional General Assembly.

- Many of the most important UN agencies and programs
have become so corrupt that they fail in their purpose, some
even to the point that they aid terrorism.

The most obviously broken pillar of the United Nations is the
General Assembly. As General Vernon Walters said when he became
the U.S. ambassador to the UN on May 13, 1985, "The United Nations
has become a place where many countries seek to achieve a lynching
of the United States by resolution." Those resolutions come from the
General Assembly.

The General Assembly

There was a memorable scene in the Japanese parliament in 2003.
Considering a resolution to send troops to participate in rebuilding
post-Saddam Iraq, the delegates debated, exchanged papers, and then
climbed over their desks and punched each other out. That model of
decorum would be an improvement for the General Assembly. Under
the UN Charter, the General Assembly is supposed to be a forum for
debate of any issues that may affect the peace and security of the world
(and for debate over the UN budget).[12] It might be able to do that if its
rules didn't allow every kakistocracy to join and vote. The UN changed
for the worse in 1968, when the Third World nations figured out that
through sheer numbers they could control the UN General Assembly
and use their majority to shakedown the United States, Britain, Japan,
and other developed nations.

They formed the "Group of 77," and in 1973, at a conference in
Algiers, under the leadership of Mexican president Luis Echeverría
Álvarez, they declared economic war on the developed nations. Eche-
verría Álvarez called for:

...a New International Economic Order that would break
the monopolies of the transnational companies of the neo-
imperialist powers.... The Third World must look on the
United States and the old imperial powers as its real enemies; the former colonies must struggle against the menace
of cultural imperialism as hard as they once struggled
against old-style imperialism; the poor countries must support the cartel of OPEC as a demonstration of Third World
power, no matter how much its price increases hurt poor
countries; the Third World must rail against injustice in two
pariahs—South Africa and Israel—and accept injustice anywhere else.[13]

That ideology was quickly and thoroughly implemented. In its infa-
mous 1975 debate, the General Assembly debated a resolution that
declared that Zionism is racism.

One of the most vocal proponents of the "Zionism is racism" resolution was Idi Amin Dada, the murderous dictator of Uganda. Speaking to the General Assembly—without a boo to be heard—Idi Amin
called for Israel's expulsion from the UN and its extermination, and
made it plain that he thought the United States was merely Israel's
tool.[14] The U.S. ambassador to the UN, Daniel Patrick Moynihan, put
this debate in perspective in a speech to the AFL-CIO:

Every day, on every side, we are assailed [at the UN]....
There are those in this country whose pleasure, or profit, it
is to believe that our assailants are motivated by what is
wrong about us. They are wrong. We are assailed because of
what is right about us. We are assailed because we are a
democracy.... It is no accident that on Wednesday His
Excellency Field Marshal Al Hadji Idi Amin Dada...called
for "the extinction of Israel as a state." And it is no accident,

I fear, that this "racist murderer"... is head of the Organization of African Unity. For Israel is a democracy and it is simply the fact that despotisms will seek whatever opportunities come to hand to destroy that which threatens them most, which is democracy.[15]

The "Zionism is racism" resolution was passed by the General Assembly by a vote of 72 to 35, with thirty-two abstentions.[16] President Ronald Reagan, in a speech to the General Assembly in 1983, told that body what its problem was: "The founders of the United Nations expected that member nations would behave and vote as individuals after they weighed the merits of an issue—rather like a great, global town meeting. The emergence of blocs and the polarization of the United Nations undermine all that this organization initially valued." The Gipper's words were pearls before swine. The game of verbally lynching the United States is still too much fun for the General Assembly members to stop.

The agenda for the General Assembly meetings in the fall of 2003 contained hundreds of resolutions concerning human rights, civil rights, and the rights of women and children (as well as one condemning the United States's 1986 raid on Libya, which was in retaliation for a Libyan bombing of a Berlin nightclub patronized by American soldiers, many of whom were killed). There were also dozens of declarations about a right to food, and other seemingly unobjectionable measures. When it came to a vote on these measures, among the "no" votes was usually the United States, and occasionally Japan and the UK. Why?

One reason is that terrorist states, following years of Soviet practice, often propose General Assembly resolutions worded in lofty terms to make political points. For example, the General Assembly passed—by a vote of 125 to 53—a resolution against applying unilateral political or economic pressure against a member state. Voting in favor were

China, Cuba, North Korea, Egypt, Iran, Libya, Sudan, Laos, Russia, Saudi Arabia, the United Arab Emirates, Vietnam, and Zimbabwe. Voting against were America, the UK, Australia, Spain, Poland, Israel, and South Korea, because these "coercive" measures isolate and weaken states that support terror and proliferate WMD.

Another reason is the UN's "agreed language" rule. Once language is "agreed to," it can be endlessly reiterated. So when the rights of Palestinian children are affirmed (in terms that require Israeli withdrawal from the West Bank), those rights are restated in virtually every new resolution. In the U.S. House of Representatives, there is a rule requiring that amendments to any bill be germane to the general purpose of the bill. In the General Assembly, there is no such requirement, so many otherwise unobjectionable resolutions are full of language condemning the United States or Israel. This is why there are so many "no" votes cast by the United States.

Typical UN Mischief: The Internet Power Grab

The General Assembly's many committees are always on the hunt for ways to create greater power in the Third World over the economies and freedoms of the developed countries. The most interesting power grab in the works seeks to impose UN control over the Internet.

The Internet—a beautifully free vehicle for freedom of speech—began in America. Not in Al Gore's head, but in the fertile minds of that most gallant gaggle of RSGs (Real Smart Guys) known as DARPA, the Defense Advanced Research Projects Agency. Over the last decade, the Internet has become a force in politics because of its ability to reach millions of people. (My Internet columns on *National Review Online* and *The American Spectator Online* regularly generate reader mail from as far away as Thailand and Australia.)

Because the Internet is controlled by the commercial market, a great many despotisms have either blocked their citizens' access to it entirely, or allow only limited access (Free countries do the opposite, which is why terrorists use Internet "cafés" all over Europe and America to communicate with each other). To fix the "problem" of Internet freedom, the UN General Assembly passed Resolution 56/183.

Resolution 56/183 provided, in seeming innocence, that a "World Summit on the Information Society" would be held to develop "a common vision and understanding of the information society and the adoption of a declaration and plan of action for implementation by Governments, international institutions and all sectors of civil society." But in the language of the UN, this means that the UN would try to take control of the Internet. The "summit" itself will be held in November 2005 in Tunisia. (So far, the costs of the preparatory talks and planning for that boondoggle already amount to $9 million.)[17]

At an earlier Geneva meeting—at which a "declaration of principles" was drafted—free press paragons Vietnam and China fought against proposals by America, Japan, Canada, and the European Union to include references to online freedom of the press and freedom of information.[18] But the free nations insisted, and thwarted the UN Internet takeover, at least for now.

The Geneva declaration of principles is instructive. It echoes language found in every UN declaration, including, of course, that the secretary-general will study the matter and refer it back to the committee. Getting along, and going along, means that the bureaucrats buy year after year of work by sending their report to the secretary-general, confident that he will send it back for more work. Occasionally, they actually do finish a product, which ends up in a treaty or a resolution that hands the United States, Japan, and Europe the bill.

Home Alone

Though, obviously, Third World delegations represent Third World ambitions, the interesting thing is that most UN delegations get to New York, set up in their plush offices, phone home—and nobody answers. Many of their governments simply forget their existence. For governments to ignore their representatives is the rule, not the exception, for members of the General Assembly. At least that's what the CIA and the KGB found out back in the days of the Gipper.

Ambassador Jose Sorzano was puzzled at the behavior of many UN delegations, so he asked the CIA to find out how many of the delegations actually received instructions from their governments on how to vote and—just for curiosity's sake—suggested to his Soviet counterpart that he do the same with the KGB. A few weeks later, they compared notes.

The spies came back with similar reports. It was a surprise, even for the most jaded UN observers. The CIA found that only thirty of the then 159 delegates were getting voting instructions from their governments. The Soviets confirmed the CIA's finding and added that, of the thirty, only two actually read the instructions (and one of those two underlined).

So the idea that the General Assembly is of vital importance to the Third World is a myth. Like the rest of us, it could get along perfectly well without the UN. The Security Council, however, is another matter entirely.

The Day the Security Council Died

The Security Council, the most powerful policy body of the UN, is composed of fifteen members. Five are permanent veto-holding members: America, the United Kingdom, China, the Russian Federation, and (sigh) France. The other ten are elected to two-year terms by the General Assembly. In early 2004, the elected ten were Chile, Germany, Pakistan, Romania, Spain, the Philippines, Algeria, Angola, Benin, and Brazil. It was in the Security Council that the French killed the UN.

President Bush had set Monday, March 10, 2003, as the deadline for UN action to authorize enforcement of its resolutions to disarm Saddam Hussein's Iraq. As that Monday dawned, French prime minister Jacques Chirac called for a later meeting of the Security Council to further debate the continued inspections of Iraq by UNMOVIC. At about 10 a.m., Colin Powell announced that the time for diplomacy had passed, and that we wouldn't even seek a UN vote on what would have been the eighteenth UN "disarm Saddam" resolution. On March 18, coalition forces slashed into Iraq.

The UN Security Council is hopelessly divided. On one side are the United States and its coalition partners, who are trying to stabilize Iraq and plant the seeds of democracy in the Middle East. On the other are the new Franco-German alliance, our Cold War enemies Russia and China, most of the Third World representatives, and an anti-American secretary-general.

It wasn't always like this—the UN Security Council, after all, was the vehicle of the "police action" to defend South Korea against Communist aggression—but the Security Council's decline into yet another anti-American forum was accelerated by two American presidents: James Earl Carter and William Jefferson Clinton.

Jimmy Carter thought the UN held America in contempt because America did wrong. So he appointed radical leftist Andrew Young as ambassador to the UN to apologize for America's many sins. Young, a civil rights lawyer and activist, criticized America for holding thousands of political prisoners, called our British allies and our Soviet foes "racists,"[19] and advocated the destruction of Western civilization, "to allow the rest of the world to really emerge as a free and brotherly society."[20] Jimmy Carter and Andrew Young made America seem weak, incompetent, and clownish in the UN.

The presidencies of Ronald Reagan and George H. W. Bush restored American prestige and even regained ground in the Security Council, which, in 1982, passed a resolution condemning Argentina's invasion of the Falkland Islands and calling for immediate withdrawal of Argentine forces.[21] Britain's forces did the rest.

Nine years later, when Saddam Hussein invaded Kuwait, the UN Security Council again responded quickly. It was clear to the United States—and to the eight other nations that co-sponsored our proposed resolution condemning Iraq's aggression—that Saddam had to be removed from Kuwait, and quickly. If he wasn't, he could have moved into the oil fields of Saudi Arabia and seized control of most of the world's oil. In an emergency meeting of the Security Council, the resolution was passed. It was the Security Council's fastest action ever to condemn aggression.[22]

But then came a new president—one who returned with much of Jimmy Carter's foreign policy team in tow. And he, like Carter, taught the Security Council and the General Assembly to believe things about American weakness and lack of resolve that simply weren't true.

CHAPTER EIGHT

CLINTON'S CLASSROOM

"Never apologize, mister. It's a sign of weakness."

—John Wayne as Captain Nathan Brittles,
She Wore a Yellow Ribbon

A SENIOR ISRAELI OFFICIAL WHO IS OFTEN ASKED TO SPEAK TO FLEDG-
ling American diplomats headed to Arab countries told me one of the
main lessons he tries to teach them is to never apologize, because the
Arabs consider it a sign of weakness. It's a lesson that William Jefferson Clinton never learned.

President Clinton had little interest in foreign policy or national
defense, and throughout his presidency apologized for one imagined
American fault after another. Clinton never understood how the levers
of American power could be pulled to move the world. Instead, because
he was so uncomfortable in his role, he was content to let others take
over for him. In the UN Security Council, and in Kofi Annan, he found
men both willing and able to do so, and he chose to let them.

Clinton sent American troops to too many places—in the interest of "peacekeeping"—yet failed to respond with decisive action to direct attacks on Americans, our embassies, and even our naval vessels. His answer to terrorist attacks was to make meaningless cruise missile strikes, and combine them with bracing speeches unconnected to policy.

When policy was important, diplomacy was disconnected, especially in the Middle East, where the Clinton administration seemed to have no clue about the signals it sent. Clinton, for instance, taught Syria that it was possible to treat American threats with casual disregard. When Warren Christopher, then secretary of state, went to Damascus to see Hafez Assad, the Syrian dictator kept him waiting for hours before condescending to meet him. Neither Christopher nor Clinton understood the diplomatic damage done by accepting that insult.

Another example was the Clinton administration's treatment of Turgut Ozal, Turkey's prime minister for many years, who had been a faithful ally in maintaining Turkey's role as a cornerstone of NATO. Our most important Muslim ally, Turkey had stood by us when Iraq invaded Kuwait in 1990. Ozal acted quickly, cutting off the Iraqi oil that flowed through Turkish pipelines, while the Arab world refused to act, seeking an "Arab solution."[1] That hurt Ozal at home, but helped us significantly by cutting off one of Saddam Hussein's principal cash flows.

When Ozal died, neither Clinton nor Vice President Gore went to the funeral. In contrast, in an administration that really cared about foreign policy, George H. W. Bush's vice president, Dan Quayle, went to so many funerals that he was labeled "ambassador to the dead." The Clinton administration's insult to a crucial ally wasn't lost on Turkey—or on the rest of the region.

In defense and foreign policy, the Clinton administration gave the appearance that it had no idea what it was doing. Clinton made America's top defense priority not fighting terrorism, but forcing liberal social experiments on the military. Clinton's first secretary of defense, former congressman Les Aspin, was an absent-minded professor. As one source who knew him well told me, "Les would walk into every morning meeting and take all of the issues we had decided the day before and toss them up in the air again. Nobody ever knew what the hell was going on, and in truth not much did."

In the midst of this chaos, Clinton decided to let the UN use American troops again and again, in places where the United States had no national interest. He believed in global "interdependence," not American sovereignty. He taught the world that America could be a tool of the UN, and that the Security Council held the reins of American power. On September 24, 1996, Clinton told the UN General Assembly:

> In this time of challenge and change, the United Nations is more important than ever before, because our world is more interdependent than ever before. Most Americans know this. Unfortunately, some Americans, in their longing to be free of the world's problems and perhaps to focus more on our own problems, ignore what the United Nations has done, ignore the benefits of cooperation, ignore our own inter-dependence with all of you in charting a better future. They ignore all the United Nations is doing to lift the lives of millions by preserving the peace, vaccinating children, caring for refugees, sharing the blessings of progress around the world. They have made it difficult for the United States to meet its obligations to the United Nations.[2]

And he told the world how America was going to fight terrorism:

> The United States is pursuing a three-part strategy against terrorists—abroad, by working more closely than ever with like-minded nations; at home, by giving our law enforcement the toughest counter-terrorism tools available, and by doing all we can to make our airports and the airplanes that link us all together even safer.[3]

There was no hint that American action could take place without UN approval. As Michael Horowitz, senior fellow at the Hudson Institute, told me, "We had a president...who really believed that you had to shackle the United States because, after all, if you didn't it would fight another Vietnam War. The president of the United States was actively involved, as a matter of foreign policy strategy, in shackling and limiting the ability of the United States to act on its own as it perceived its own interest to be." As Horowitz said, Clinton would "see a problem, talk about it, sign a piece of paper, declare victory, and move on to the next problem, and leave the underlying issues festering."

From Haiti to Kosovo, American troops were put in the service of the UN, not in the service of the United States. Worst of all was Somalia.

Clinton's Somalia intervention made almost every conceivable mistake. It followed—almost immediately—the withdrawal of American troops sent there by George H. W. Bush under an earlier UN resolution.

In 1992, after his defeat by Clinton, Bush sent twenty-five thousand American soldiers and Marines to help distribute food to starving Somalis and to protect aid workers from murderous Somali warlords. Bush's ambassador, Robert Oakley, arranged a cease-fire between the principal warlords, Mohamed Farah Aideed and Ali Mahdi Mohamed.[4]

The Americans succeeded in calming the situation, their presence sufficient to drive the fighters out of the major city of Mogadishu. UN secretary-general Boutros Boutros-Ghali of Egypt wasn't satisfied, however, and insisted that the Americans disarm the warlords and their troops. Bush refused, and Boutros-Ghali agreed to his demand that a UN force replace the Americans.[5] Maybe it was because Bush knew that Boutros-Ghali had an old personal score to settle with Aideed; Boutros-Ghali had worked against Aideed while serving as an Egyptian diplomat in Siad Barre's Somalia.[6] Whatever the reason, Bush didn't allow the UN to take control of American troops or their orders. Most of the Americans were withdrawn by the time the UN forces—a conglomeration of troops from thirty-three countries—took their place. But the UN force, though much larger than the original American troop deployment, proved unable to handle the warlords, and chaos returned. President Clinton sent American troops back to Somalia for a brief and disastrous time.

The Defeat of Task Force Ranger

On the afternoon of October 3, 1993, a U.S. force took off by helicopter to capture Aideed. Major General Jim Garrison, the U.S. Army commander in Somalia, had asked for Abrams tanks and Bradley fighting vehicles to bolster the strength of his fighting forces, but was turned down by Les Aspin's Pentagon.[7] The raiding force—composed of Army Rangers and Delta Force operators—was some of the best we have. A rocket-propelled grenade brought down a Black Hawk helicopter, setting in motion a battle in the streets of Mogadishu that raged through that night and most of the next day. The fight dragged on because Garrison had no tanks or heavy vehicles that could penetrate blocked streets and incessant fire where the helicopter had gone down. Pakistani and Malaysian troops—who had tanks and armored vehicles—took hours to decide if they would brave the streets of Mogadishu to rescue the trapped Americans.

Eighteen Americans died in the battle and dozens were wounded. Television footage showed a howling mob dragging the body of a dead American soldier through the streets. Two days later, Clinton announced a reinforcement of the Somalia deployment, this time—he said—under American command.[8] He didn't even know the original force had been under Garrison's command. Shortly thereafter, Clinton announced that American troops would withdraw from Somalia by March 1994.

Clinton taught terrorists exactly the wrong lesson at Mogadishu, and his feckless policies repeated it, again and again.

What It Means to the Soldier

The day after the battle, my friend Dale McClellan, then a young Navy SEAL operator, landed in Mogadishu. He told me, "They were still washing the blood out of the Humvees when we got there." Images of American bodies being lugged through the streets were burned into his mind. Then he began learning some of the very hard realities of UN "peacekeeping" in the Clinton administration. Rules of engagement banned any offensive action; the accepted protocol was just to "shoot only if you're being shot at."

Spend my life if you have to, but don't waste it is part of the warrior's creed. In Somalia, however, lives were spent, but there was no intention of seeing the job through.

"I have a hard time explaining this to my mom," McClellan told me. "But it means everything to the soldiers, and their families. I talked a lot with the senior enlisted guys and some of our officers while I was in Somalia. They always asked, 'Why the hell are we here?' It seemed pointless. We knew the place was going to go back to what it was before we came.... Who wants to waste his life on something like that?" He puts it very well: "The least they can do is finish the job we went over there for. We never did that in UN peacekeeping missions. All those men died in Somalia, but what for?" As McClellan sees it, under President Bush, the bond between soldier and president has been restored. "I can go over there [to Iraq or Afghanistan] with a bunch of twenty-two-year-old kids or forty-year-old men, and we'd go with a smile, because there's a reason to be there. And we're not leaving until the job is done. That means everything to the men who fight, and the families of the men who die there."

By teaching the world that the United States would spend the lives of its soldiers pursuing the UN's interests—not its own—Clinton told our soldiers that their lives were of less value to him than the empty praise he received from Kofi Annan and the UN. He thus broke the bond that American warriors hold most sacred: a commander in chief's commitment to hold his soldiers' lives in trust.

Commander in Chief Kofi Annan

In 1995, Clinton—undeterred by the Somalia debacle—deployed American troops under UN command to Macedonia. One of those ordered to go was Specialist Michael New. New had no problem with going to Macedonia, but he had a big problem with the order that every soldier serving under UN command would wear the UN blue helmet, and that the U.S. flag patch on the right shoulder—by tradition, the most important on the uniform—would be removed and replaced by the UN flag, badge, and insignia. The U.S. flag was demoted to the left side. New refused, was court-martialed, and was sentenced to a bad conduct discharge. The court's choice was either to find New guilty or to find Clinton guilty of wrongly placing U.S. troops under UN command. The rest of the troops complied with the order, but the bitterness over that incident—and the distrust between the commander in chief and the troops—never faded.[9] Clinton's goal was achieved: America's subordination to the UN was clear.

Addressing the nation on November 27, 1995, Clinton talked about the UN intervention in Bosnia:

> When I took office, some were urging immediate intervention in the conflict. I decided that American ground troops should not fight a war in Bosnia because the United States could not force peace on Bosnia's warring ethnic groups.... But as months of war turned into years, it became clear that Europe alone could not end the conflict.

Clinton never explained what American interests were implicated in the Bosnian civil war. By the end of his presidency, Bill Clinton had reformed the world's image of America, and not for the better. There are three lessons he taught the global community:

- The UN, by determining where American forces should go, can be an effective means of constraining the United States in the exercise of its power.
- America will not respond decisively when it is attacked. Clinton took no decisive action in retaliation for the 1993 World Trade Center bombing, the 1996 Khobar Tower bombing in Saudi Arabia, the 1998 attacks on our embassies in Africa, or the 2000 attack on the USS *Cole*.

- Inflicting only a few casualties on the United States, as in
  Somalia, can defeat the United States.

These lessons, as the world has discovered since September 11, 2001, are false. One of the principal reasons we face the opposition we do today—in the UN, in Iraq, and in Europe—is that for eight long years, the world was taught to expect that America would subordinate its national interests to some other body, something America has—for almost 228 years—refused to do.

Today, we are paying a huge cost in blood and treasure to make the world unlearn what it was taught in the Clinton years.

CHAPTER NINE

UN REFORM: A FOOL'S ERRAND

*"There are many cases in which the United Nations has
failed....Justice cannot be a hit-or-miss system.
We cannot be content with an arrangement where
our system of international laws apply only to those
who are willing to keep them."*

—Winston Churchill

ON NOVEMBER 4, 2003, SECRETARY-GENERAL KOFI ANNAN ANNOUNCED a "high-level" panel to examine global threats and the UN itself, and to recommend whatever changes the panel believed were necessary to "ensure effective collective action, including but not limited to a review of the principal organs of the United Nations."[1] The panel is composed of representatives from France, Brazil, Norway, Ghana, Australia, the United Kingdom, Uruguay, Egypt, India, Japan, Russia, China, Pakistan, Tanzania, and the United States. The panel will labor for months and produce a mouse. Or, more likely, a rat. Annan has already told the panel what he wants: a Third World country, probably from among the Arab states, to become a permanent veto-holding member of the Security Council. This would make Security Council action against terrorists and the countries that support them impossible.

The bottom line is: Trying to fix the UN is a fool's errand, because in order to fix the UN, you need the cooperation of the states that are the problem. Some people, such as former ambassador Max Kampelman, argue that we should reform the UN by creating a new organization within it. In a January 6, 2004, op-ed in the *Wall Street Journal*, Kampelman wrote, "At a minimum, it is essential that the U.S. take the lead in establishing and strengthening a Caucus of Democratic States committed to advancing the UN's assigned role for world peace, human dignity and democracy."[2]

But this is pie in the sky. Let's say we formed a "democracy caucus" in the UN. It could be made up of the NATO member states, Israel, Japan, and a few other countries. And suppose we proposed an amendment to the UN Charter barring state sponsors of terror like Iran and Syria from chairing any UN organizations, including the Human Rights Commission and the Disarmament Commission. Suppose we also, as part of this amendment, barred the election of any state onto the Security Council (as a non-permanent member) without approval of the "democracy caucus." That would be real progress.

But such an amendment would have to be passed by a two-thirds vote of the General Assembly and ratified by a two-thirds vote of the Security Council, including unanimous support from the five permanent members.[3] Saddam Hussein has a better chance of returning to power than our resolution would have in passing the General Assembly and the Security Council. Of the 191 members of the UN, fifty, at most, have some claim to be democratic. And very few Third World, or even European, members of the UN want to give up what they think they have: a way to control the power of the United States.

British historian Corelli Barnett said in a letter to me that membership in the League of Nations in the 1930s bound Britain to take military action even where British interests were not at all threatened. In contrast, Barnett said:

> In 2003 the UN has the reverse function in regard to the
> US—to restrain it from taking action. From the perspective

of Europe, Russia, China and from public opinion even in countries whose governments support Bush's Washington (e.g., Britain and Spain), this potential ability to restrain the US is now the chief virtue of the UN.

Barnett's view is consistent with many who confuse the concepts of multilateralism with commitment to the UN and the need for, as Howard Dean put it, the UN's "permission" for U.S. action. America cannot and should not be isolationist, but that doesn't mean that we have to be multilateralist in the sense UN members want us to be.

The world's most vocal multilateralist is France's president, Jacques Chirac. His view is that the UN should hold sway over diplomatic and military action because without the UN, there is only the "anarchy of a society without rules."[4] His speech to the UN General Assembly in the aftermath of the Iraq campaign sets this out very clearly. Chirac speaks for the international elite that believes the UN has—as Barnett described—the proper role of constraining the United States:

> The United Nations has just weathered one of its most serious trials in its history: respect for the Charter, the use of force, were at the heart of the [Iraq] debate. The war, which was started without the authorization of the Security Council, has shaken the multilateral system.[5]

Chirac wants the world to believe that any action America takes is illegitimate without UN authorization. But Article 1, Section 8 of the United States Constitution gives Congress, not the United Nations, the power to declare war—a sovereign right that few Americans want to surrender.

In 1996, Senator Jesse Helms of North Carolina sounded an urgent warning about the UN:

> The international elites running the United Nations look at the idea of the nation-state with disdain; they consider it a

discredited notion of the past that has been superseded by
the idea of the United Nations. In their view, the interests of
the nation-states are parochial and should give way to the
global interests. Nation-states, they believe, should recognize
the primacy of these global interests and accede to the
United Nations' sovereignty to pursue them.[6]

Unfortunately, much of Europe seems to have taken the side of these
"international elites." So the West is divided. Underlying this division
is a strong element of anti-Americanism in Europe.

British member of Parliament John Redwood has been called the
Conservative Party's "lean, mean, thinking machine." He told me, "I
do think the west is very disunited, largely because the principal engines
of the EU are anti-American. In addition, old national divisions, and
the traditional antipathy of the periphery for the centre in Europe create additional tensions. That is why the USA finds the EU so disap-
pointing when it has something important to do, like the war on
terrorism."

The West is split between a continental Western Europe that sees the
world only in terms of trade and commerce—and that accepts terrorism as a part of life to be dealt with by law enforcement—and the
United States, Britain, and the few other serious nations that see radical Islamic terrorism as a global threat as dangerous as Communism.
The Europeans who are in denial about this have rendered the UN
Security Council useless. In the words of Margaret Thatcher:

For years, many governments played down the threats of
Islamic revolution, turned a blind eye to international ter-
rorism and accepted the development of weaponry of mass
destruction. Indeed, some politicians were happy to go fur-
ther, collaborating with the self-proclaimed enemies of the
West for their own short-term gain—but enough about the
French. So deep has the rot set in that the UN Security
Council itself was paralyzed.[7]

And that is where it stands today. The UN Security Council is paralyzed by the disunity of the Western nations. The future of the Security Council was defined when France and Russia, owed billions of dollars from Iraq and eager to collect on sweetheart oil contracts they had negotiated with Saddam Hussein's regime, prevented any Security Council approval of action to enforce the resolutions they had previously condoned.

In short, the Security Council is broken beyond repair. America then has to face the question: What is our proper role in the UN from here forward?

Getting Out of the UN Game

A partial solution to the UN problem would be to get it to leave America. On September 20, 1983, America's ambassador to the United Nations, Charles Lichtenstein, suggested just that:

> If in the judicious determination of the members of the United Nations they feel they are not welcome and treated with the hostly consideration that is their due, the United States strongly encourages member states to seriously consider removing themselves and this organization from the soil of the United States. We will put no impediment in your way. The members of the U.S. mission to the United Nations will be down at the dockside waving you a fond farewell as you sail off into the sunset.

As nice a thought as UN departure might be, it won't happen. The UN building in New York City is owned by the UN and is regarded as international soil, so we can't just tell them we're taking it back and toss them out. They won't move—even temporarily—and we can't force them to.

But one thing we can do is end our UN membership. Indeed, that's what British historian Paul Johnson told me: "America should leave the UN and start from scratch with the democratic and law-abiding states." He added, "This might succeed because many nations would like an alternative to the viciousness and incapacity of the UN."

Johnson is right, but we can't simply walk out. America needs time to wean the free nations of the world away from the UN and into the new forum. To do this, we should withdraw from the UN gradually, in stages, and build on the growing UN disillusion in European, and even global, popular opinion (if not the opinion of European and Third World governments).

In its latest survey of world opinion, the Pew Foundation interviewed people in twenty-one nations, including ten in Europe. It found that:

> While there is a growing consensus that the UN has become less relevant, overall positive opinions of the world body have also decreased. The percentage of people who say the UN has a good influence on their country has declined in nations that took military action against Iraq—including Great Britain and the US—as well as those that bitterly opposed the war. Positive views of the UN dropped by 37 percentage points in Great Britain and 29 points in the US; the negative change was nearly as sharp in Germany (33 points) and France (28 points).[8]

To further this political climate change against the UN, we must end the pretense of UN control over the important issues facing the free world: weapons proliferation, terrorism, and the economies of the free nations.

First and foremost, no American president should ever again bring any serious issue before the UN Security Council. Consideration of any action we and our allies choose to take to defeat global terrorism is not a proper subject for UN debate. The Security Council and the secretary-general have to be made to realize that in our eyes—and in the eyes of the world—legitimacy comes from the rightness of the cause, not the blessing of the fifteen members of the Security Council.

Second, we could reduce the rank of our representative. Now, America's representative holds the rank of full ambassador, the equal of our representatives to real nations. Any representation of the United States in the UN should be by someone of lower rank. By reducing the rank of our representative, we reduce the UN's importance.

Third, we must shut off all U.S. funding for the UN—every penny—until the Iraq Oil-for-Food program is investigated to our satisfaction and the new Iraq Development Fund set up to prevent it from becoming just as corrupt as its predecessor. The entire UN—from Secretary-General Annan on down—should be investigated and any corruption revealed. Once that is done, anyone who has participated in the corruption—anyone—must be fired and charges against him or her brought in whatever court may have jurisdiction. The investigation and subsequent legal action cannot be taken under the aegis of any UN organization (including the International Court of Justice) because these organizations cannot be trusted to be impartial.

Fourth, we should take direct action against UN organizations such as UNRWA (which is a front for terror) that do active harm. A Security Council resolution (never mind that it won't pass) should be introduced, and a debate forced, on the matter of removing the heads of those agencies, starting with UNRWA's Peter Hansen, in order to expose what these agencies actually do and remove their credibility.

Fifth, we must insist that the next secretary-general—and all subsequent secretary-generals—be from successful, free, and capitalist nations; support democracy and human rights and oppose terror; and not come from the UN bureaucracy. Kofi Annan's term expires in 2006, and we are constrained by the UN rules on electing a successor. The UN Charter provides that the secretary-general is appointed by the General Assembly on the basis of a recommendation from the Security Council.[9] Tradition says that the secretary-generalship rotates around the world's regions and that no native of a permanent member of the Security Council can be secretary-general. Annan is from Africa. Before him, we had an Egyptian, a Peruvian, a Burmese, and three Europeans.

So the next secretary-general is expected to come from an Asian or Pacific nation.

Some conservatives want a secretary-general who will cast aside any vestiges of UN authority by his radicalism. It's not hard to imagine former Malaysian premier Mahathir bin Mohamad—Third World radical and anti-Semite—serving to sever even some of the world's elites' attachment to the UN. But this isn't the right course. We need to remember that the objective is to minimize the damage the UN can cause while we move ourselves and our allies into a new framework for international cooperation.

We should search, now, in countries like Japan, India, Singapore, and Turkey, to find candidates who share our values and who could help the UN regain a sense of reality.

New Alliances of the Free

If America is to lead the free nations out of the UN, we need first to define where we are going, and how we can get there. Our destination should be a new global organization of the free and democratic nations with which we share values and goals.

The new organization we establish must be outside of the UN, and be open to all nations that allow their people the basic freedoms of religion, press, assembly, and the others we cherish.

The new organization should not be created as a military alliance. Its goal would be to do what the UN was created to do, but is incapable of doing. We—and the other founders of this new global forum— can fix the problems of the UN from the start in a new charter. Such a charter should be based, as NATO's charter was, on the Atlantic Charter devised by Roosevelt and Churchill. The eight points of the Atlantic Charter (minus the sixth, which dealt specifically with the defeat of Nazi Germany) would be the starting principles of the new organization. In a form modified to deal with the threats posed not just by nations, but by non-state actors such as terrorists and their sponsors, the first principles of the new charter should be the members' agreement to the following:

- To seek no aggrandizement, territorial or otherwise
- To condemn territorial changes that do not accord with the freely expressed wishes of the peoples concerned
- To respect the right of all peoples to choose the form of government under which they will live; and to wish to see sovereign rights and self-government restored to those who have been forcibly deprived of such
- To endeavor, with due respect for their existing obligations, to further the enjoyment by all nations, great or small, of equal access to trade and to the raw materials of the world needed for their economic prosperity
- To work toward the fullest collaboration among all nations in the economic field, with the object of securing improved labor standards and economic advancements for all
- To enable all people to traverse the high seas, the sky, and outer space without hindrance
- To commit to the belief that all the nations and people of the world, for realistic as well as spiritual reasons, must come to the abandonment of the use of force. Since no future peace can be achieved or maintained if land, sea, or air armaments continue to be employed by nations and non-state actors which threaten aggression outside their frontiers, members must believe that pending the establishment of a wider and permanent system of general security, that the disarmament of such nations and non-state actors is essential, and the proliferation of weapons of denial and mass destruction must be interdicted and ended.[10] Members will likewise aid and encourage all other practicable measures that will lighten for peace-loving peoples the crushing burden of armaments.

The new charter would add an article aimed at the realities of changing governments, terrorism, and proliferation of missiles and other weapons and technology:

- To believe that the inequality of nations results not only from size, wealth, and military strength, but from the inequality of freedoms nations allow their peoples. Therefore, nations that allow the essential, God-given, fundamental human rights of freedom of religion, speech, security of the person and trial by jury, due process of law, the press, assembly, and the protection against cruel and unusual punishments, shall be entitled to membership. No nation shall, by virtue of the rights granted by its government at any one time, be entitled to retain membership if, in the judgment of the founding members, a successor government fails to ensure and protect these fundamental rights.

These beginnings of a charter establish a predicate for global cooperation without the indelible defects in the UN Charter. This charter would discriminate—openly and properly—against nations that fail to provide the basic human rights on which our nation was founded. It enables the member nations to consider seriously problems dealing only with peace and resistance to aggression in all forms, both of states and terrorists. It also provides the basis for establishing trade agreements among nations. This alone will be a powerful incentive to join, especially for nations such as Turkey that have been discriminated against by other non-UN alliances (e.g., the EU).

Gaining acceptance of this charter, and gathering members of the new organization, will take much time and effort. Every nation that joins cannot be required to first give up its membership in the UN. But gradually, as the organization gains adherents, and proves its usefulness in the ways the UN cannot, it will grow. And the UN will shrink in importance and in size.

President Bush has already begun the process of establishing an alternative to the UN. In December 2002, the president announced a "National Strategy to Combat Weapons of Mass Destruction." This strategy is aimed at preventing the proliferation of WMD, taking direct action to prevent it, and building the capacity to deal with an attack on America employing nuclear, chemical, or biological weapons. It states, in part, "The United States will actively employ diplomatic approaches in bilateral and multilateral settings in pursuit of our non-proliferation roles." Such diplomacy can't, and won't, take place in the UN.

Part of the National Strategy was to take active measures to disrupt, disable, or destroy WMD en route to their targets. "This requires," it said, "capabilities to detect and destroy an adversary's WMD assets before these weapons are used." President Bush's opponents scoff at his diplomacy. Senator John Kerry said, "Our diplomacy has been about as arrogant and ineffective as anything that I have ever seen." But the president's diplomacy has succeeded where the UN has failed, and was accomplished outside the reach of Annan and the Security Council. The result—after barely a year—includes the WMD disarmament of one terrorist nation: Libya.

In May 2003, President Bush announced the Proliferation Security Initiative (PSI), under which eleven nations have agreed to work outside the UN to correct one of the gravest problems the world now faces: the proliferation of missiles, missile technology, and WMD.

The UN's efforts in arms control are a clear failure. North Korea, for example, had only one significant export in the past decade: missiles. It sells to all comers, and has already armed rogue nations such as Iran. Pakistan—a putative ally of the United States—has also been exporting nuclear weapons technology. Libya, we now know, was far along in developing nuclear weapons before it decided to disarm. The UN has failed in every case.

President Bush's initiative, on the other hand, is already working. Without UN permission or debate, the eleven member states of the PSI are stopping shipments—from North Korea and other outlaw states—of missiles and other weapons on the high seas, in the air, and on the ground.

The PSI nations are Australia, Japan, Poland, Portugal, Spain, the United Kingdom, the United States, France, Germany, the Netherlands, and Italy. On September 23, 2003, President Bush informed the UN that the PSI states would do the job independently of the UN. He told the General Assembly:

> Through our Proliferation Security Initiative, eleven nations are preparing to search planes and ships, trains and trucks carrying suspect cargo, and to seize weapons or missile shipments that raise proliferation concerns. These nations have agreed on a set of interdiction principles, consistent with current legal authorities. And we're working to expand the Proliferation Security Initiative to other countries. We're determined to keep the world's most destructive weapons away from all our shores, and out of the hands of our common enemies.

Deputy Secretary of Defense Paul Wolfowitz told me that the PSI's catching Libya "in a violation, a major violation" of non-proliferation agreements has been "a crucial part of our success" in convincing Libya to end and surrender its WMD program.

On March 15, 2004, Energy Secretary Spence Abraham displayed for the press some of the nuclear weapons materials "recovered" from Libya. Among the items Abraham displayed were four "P1" aluminum centrifuge casings standing more than five and a half feet tall, and "cascade" piping, which he called "the main circuitry that connects all of the centrifuges." Other centrifuges were still in their wooden crates. One box shipped from Libya was marked "FRAGILE."[11]

Abraham said Libya's program included a "formidable" four thousand centrifuges. A centrifuge is a rapidly rotating cylinder that can be used to enrich uranium for use as nuclear bomb fuel. Libya's ultimate objective was to have as many as ten thousand centrifuges operating.

Much of what Abraham displayed, according to another Defense Department source, wasn't surrendered by Libya. Acting as part of the PSI interdiction campaign, the Italians searched a Libyan-bound ship that docked briefly in Italy; the nuclear materials were discovered and seized.

After the seizure, American diplomats told Libyan dictator Muammar Qadafi that the game was up for his nuclear program. Caught red-handed, and fearing military action, Qadafi decided to disarm, and then agreed to ship the rest of his nuclear weapons materials to America. This is a huge success for the PSI, and for every nation that is our partner in it.

Upon this foundation other specific action-oriented initiatives can be built that will make the world safer and move other nations to cooperate outside of the UN. With each of these initiatives, the free and responsible nations of the world will become accustomed to working outside the UN, and the UN will be left for what it is—a home for despots and bureaucrats.

CHAPTER TEN

THE DEATH OF OLD EUROPE

*"Heaven is a place where the chefs are Italian, the police
are British, the lovers French, the mechanics German and
everything is run by the Swiss. In Hell, the chefs are British,
the police German, the lovers Swiss, the mechanics French,
and everything is run by the Italians."*

—German ambassador Immo Stabreit

WELCOME TO EUROPE'S SELF-IMPOSED HELL, THE EUROPEAN UNION. IF
the PSI is an example of effective international cooperation, the EU is
an example of how Old Europe is killing itself, and why it has accelerated the worst trends in the UN.

The EU began life as a free-trade zone, metastasized into a pseudo-
state, and seeks a status it cannot achieve: equality with the United
States in both economic and military power. It will not achieve either,
because Europe is dying. Its economies are sclerotic and sinking under
the socialist policies they have followed for decades. As Czech president
Vaclav Havel said, "Europeans are living in a 'dream world' of welfare
and long vacations," and have yet to realize that "they are not moving
toward some sort of nirvana."[1]

Each year, the Heritage Foundation publishes the *Index of Economic Freedom*,[2] which catalogues the nations of the world by factors including trade policy, the fiscal burden of government, government intervention in the economy, and regulation. It rates each nation on its degree of economic freedom and rank in the world. Its conclusions on the major EU nations tell all.

France and Germany—whose populations comprise about 60 percent of the whole EU population—are sinking fast. According to Heritage:

> France remains a relatively statist country. Public expenditures amounted to 52.6 percent of the GDP in 2001, and the state employees 25 percent of the workforce, double the percentage in both Germany and the United Kingdom. Most notoriously, since February 2000, the legal workweek has been a miniscule 35 hours for firms of more than 20 workers.... At present, 10 workers support four pensioners; by 2040 those same 10 workers will be forced to support seven pensioners.[3]

The combined burden of the pensioners, regulations, and socialist policies leaves France only "mostly free" economically, according to Heritage. It also leaves France with a dying economy. Germany is even worse. It, like France, is "mostly free" economically. As Heritage shows, it's also an economic basket case.

> Germany has both the largest and the weakest economy in the European Union. In the 10 years ending in 2001, annual GDP growth averaged just 1.5 percent.... Germany's economic problems cannot be explained primarily by the global economic slow-down, as Germany has been affected far more than its Western peers; rather, the answer lies in the country's structural problems. Non-wage labor costs are

equal to a staggeringly high 42 percent of gross wages. Fundamental economic reform of Germany's welfare and labor market systems has become imperative.[4]

Germany's economy, like France's, is being eaten away by socialism, and the EU is accelerating its fall. British Conservative Party leader Michael Howard opposes Britain's joining in the common euro currency, and cites Germany as the best evidence for his position. Howard told me, "The most important instrument any country has, in the sense of influencing its economic policy, is its control over interest rates. You really have to look at the attention paid to the decisions of the Federal Reserve or the Bank of England or the European Central Bank. I see absolutely no reason why we should give up that key measure of control. I'm not particularly a critic of the European Central Bank because I think it has an impossible job to do. It has to fix a single interest rate for twelve countries whose economies are pursuing widely different courses. The consequence of that is that its interest rates are too high for some and too low for others and about right for very few."

I asked Howard if his view would be different if France and Germany hadn't violated the EU debt ceiling of 3 percent. He said, "My view is quite independent of that. The economies have different needs. The European economy is not a single economy. If you look at Germany for example, there is little doubt that the difficulties which the German economy has recently experienced would have been considerably mitigated if they had been able to set their own interest rates."

Italy is no better. Its pension liabilities—15 percent of its GDP—are the highest in Europe.[5] According to the *Index*, "Belgium has one of Western Europe's most punishing tax systems, and one of the world's highest total tax burdens."[6] Denmark is also following the socialist path, making it "a large welfare state with high taxes."[7]

The EU is based on a false premise. It is attempting to combine fifteen—soon to be twenty-five—weak economies with the objective of establishing an economic superpower. And it is doing so without first correcting the socialist policies that are driving their economies into the ground. As Dr. John Hulsman, research fellow and senior policy analyst for Europe at the Heritage Foundation, told me, "It's even worse than that."

Hulsman said, "Here's a statistic that makes my hair go white. According to the OECD—which is a pro-European organization—since 1970 in Western Europe there's been a net private sector job loss. This is a staggering statistic. When Europeans tell us that we have a different economic system from them—they assume some moral equivalence—the reality is that their system is not working in a fundamental way."

There are a couple of success stories. Under its conservative government, Spain was privatizing, cutting red tape, and growing economically. But in March 2004, in reaction to the al-Qaeda bombing of Spain's railways on March 11, the Spanish elected a socialist government that could undo Spain's economic progress. Ireland, according to Hulsman, has a per capita GDP higher than the UK for the first time in history. Why? "The Irish have done a couple of things brilliantly. They have one of the lowest corporate tax rates in the world, they have a low personal income tax rate, and they have a highly educated work force," said Hulsman.

"The problem is that harmonization in the European Union is never downward, meaning nobody ever says, 'Let's adopt as a uniform measure Ireland's tax rate.' Rather, they say—and the French use the term—'unfair economic advantage,' meaning lower taxes. If they agree on concrete uniformities, it's always to the French and German level in an effort, of course, to make their moribund economies competitive by making other states drop their competitive advantages."

By joining themselves in the EU, these nations can't create an economic superpower. Instead, the EU will doom all its members to stagnation and economic failure. So will the fact that the French are too busy puffing on their Galois to reproduce.

Almost 10 percent of France's population is Islamic. If the immigrant population continues to reproduce much faster than the native population (which is not reproducing at parity with the death rate), France could have an Islamic majority in about fifty years. So could other European countries. Among the many false premises on which the European Union is based, one is that Europe will remain demographically European, without having to assimilate a large and fast-growing Muslim population.

As John Hulsman put it, "The problem for the French is that unlike the United States, which has an unparalleled record of assimilation, the French assimilation is much more uniform and rigid. The French say that you're only truly French and can reap the economic benefits of being French—and be taken seriously socially—if you adopt all French mores, customs, including the French language and have absolutely no deviation from what France sees as its self-image. As a result, these Muslim communities have not assimilated at all and around every major French city are suburbs dominated by Muslims with a population...of very frustrated younger people, many of them without work. French unemployment in the ages eighteen to twenty-four, when you should just be starting to enter the workforce, is about 20 percent."

In late 2003, France's irrepressibly repressive President Chirac proposed a new law banning Muslim women from wearing headscarves in French schools. In an attempt to appear balanced, the proposed law also bans the wearing of yarmulkes—the Jewish religious cap—and "overly large" Christian crosses by school students. In January 2004, Sikhs were informed that their young men could not wear turbans to school, which effectively bans them from French schools.[8] This new law passed the lower house of the French parliament in February and is expected to go into effect in September 2004. It will push Muslim students out of French public schools, and into private Muslim schools, negating the most useful social tool of assimilation: the education of the young.

Hulsman added, "You have angry young Muslim men who are not being given social or economic opportunities, sitting there jobless day upon day." There are riots waiting to happen around every major French city.

In a century or less, France will not be French, which, surprisingly, is not necessarily good news, if it becomes instead a radical Islamic power. America need not be concerned with the "global economic superpower" that the EU fancies itself. But we must be concerned about the anti-Americanism that infects so much of it, and which is getting worse.

Anti-American Europe

L'Effroyable Imposture, a book by French author Thierry Meyssan, was on the French bestseller list for six weeks in 2002. The title—*The Horrifying Fraud* in English—introduces the author's incredible assertion that the September 11, 2001, attacks on America were carried out by the U.S. government to create an excuse to attack Afghanistan and Iraq. Meyssan wrote that no aircraft hit the Pentagon, rather, explosives were planted on the ground. According to the book, the aircraft that hit the World Trade Center were piloted by remote control, not al-Qaeda terrorists. Meyssan's book broke the record for first-month sales in France, beating the record previously held by Madonna's *Sex*.

Europe's anti-Americanism is both wide and deep. It's also very hard to understand except in terms of envy and of Europe's own weaknesses and fears. French author Jean-Francois Revel describes the consistent drumbeat of the Euro elites all too well:

> Strangely, it is always America that is described as degenerate and "fascist," while it is solely in Europe that actual dictatorships and totalitarian regimes spring up.... On the whole, American society is sweepingly condemned as practically the worst association of human beings in history.... Why is the USA casually accused of "fascism" when it is a land that has never known a dictator over the course of two centuries, while Europe has been busy making troops of them?[9]

European elites consider themselves superior to Americans in history, culture, and "maturity," but this is just a thick layer of hypocrisy covering Europe's disdain for America.

President Bush's policy of preemption against terrorists—if you believe the Euro elites—is an aberration created by a reckless cowboy president. But preemption is anything but new. When it was applied for Europe's direct benefit, Europe was glad of it. Three months before Pearl Harbor—ironically, on September 11, 1941—President Roosevelt said:

> I assume that the German leaders are not deeply concerned... by what we Americans or the American Government say or publish about them. We cannot bring about the downfall of Nazism by the use of long-range invective. But when you see a rattlesnake poised to strike, you do not wait until he has struck before you crush him.
>
> These Nazi submarines and raiders are the rattlesnakes of the Atlantic. They are a menace to the free pathways of the high seas. They are a challenge to our sovereignty. They hammer at our most precious rights when they attack ships of the American flag....
>
> It is clear to all Americans that the time has come when the Americas themselves must now be defended. A continuation of attacks in our own waters, or in waters that could be used for further and greater attacks on us, will inevitably weaken our American ability to repel Hitlerism.
>
> Do not let us be Hairsplitters. Let us not ask ourselves whether the Americas should begin to defend themselves after the first attack, or the fifth attack, or the tenth attack, or the twentieth attack.
>
> The time for active defense is now.... This is the time for prevention of attack.

If submarines or raiders attack in distant waters, they can attack equally well within sight of our own shores. Their very presence in any waters which America deems vital to its defense constitutes an attack.

In the waters which we deem necessary for our defense, American naval vessels and American planes will no longer wait until Axis submarines lurking under the water, or Axis raiders on the surface of the sea, strike their deadly blow—first.[10]

The European elites cannot get around the simple fact that—despite what Bill Clinton led them to believe—we aren't them, and we don't deal with the world the way they do. We all want to be prosperous, but only the EU, not the U.S., sees advantages in trading with terrorist states.

A good recent example is the EU's relationship with Syria. Damascus is awash in Islamic terrorism. Its meeting places are like a terrorist union hiring hall. Virtually every known Islamic terrorist group operates in and from Syria. Many, including Hamas and Hezbollah, have facilities from which they operate openly. And in 2003, when Syria was sending arms and fighters into Iraq to oppose the military campaign, the EU was negotiating a trade agreement with Syria.

Syria, moreover, is one of the principal forces behind the insurgency in post-Saddam Iraq. Syrian money, arms, and men still seep into Iraq to prevent democracy from taking root. By the time Saddam Hussein's regime fell, billions of dollars looted from Iraq had been deposited in Syrian banks. At this writing, in the spring of 2004, Syria has refused to surrender the money to the new Iraqi government.

By December 2003, the EU was announcing success in its Syrian negotiation. EU trade commissioner Pascal Lamy said:

This is an important stepping-stone in our long established goal of creating a Euro-Mediterranean free trade area. This agreement will help Syria better integrate into the world economy and paves the way for other initiatives, including possible future membership of the World Trade Organization.[11]

The EU is allying itself with Syria in the same way two of its members—France and Germany—were allied with Saddam's Iraq: as a trade partner and patron in the UN.

Just as France and Germany opposed toppling Saddam Hussein, we must now expect that the EU nations will oppose any effort to topple, or even pressure, Syria's dictator, Bashar Assad; it also tells the world that the EU nations will not join America in fighting terrorists and the nations that support them.

America sees terrorism as an existential threat, one that is aimed at ending our way of life. The EU nations prefer to see that threat as something much less, and refuse even to reduce their economic partnership with terrorist nations.

Old Europe's values and goals are no longer consistent with ours. General Joe Ralston saw it at the highest level, first as head of European command and as Wesley Clark's successor as NATO chief.[12]

As Ralston explained it, "There is a greater cultural gap than what Americans are normally accustomed to. The most divisive issue that I ran into at every reception or cocktail party, no matter the level of sophistication, was the death penalty. The Europeans couldn't believe that the Americans could still be so barbaric as to have a death penalty. And to most Americans, this is not even an issue. During the election campaign of 2000 people would come up to me and say they couldn't believe Governor Bush was even a serious candidate because so many people had been put to death in Texas. They don't understand that over there."

This lack of understanding is found at every level. According to the *London Times*, Cherie Blair—wife of Prime Minister Tony Blair—accosted President Bush about the death penalty during a presidential visit to Britain.[13]

Ralston said, "There is a much greater difference in values—which may not be the right term. For example, the Kyoto [global warming] Treaty. I believe the president did the right thing, because it's a flawed treaty. But people don't want to get into the issues over there. To them, well, you're just anti-environment."

Ralston made a very unusual point. In the United States, there is constant dialogue between the military and Congress, often to the discomfiture of the White House. That same communication doesn't exist in Europe, and it accounts for many of the European political decisions, which seem, on the surface, perfectly anti-military. But, as Ralston explained, those decisions are made more from ignorance than antipathy.

He told me, "Take the International Criminal Court. I spent a lot of time on that. That is a terribly flawed concept. Let's take an American soldier. And he's accused of a war crime. In our system, he'd be investigated, you'd have an Article 32[14] and it would go on to court-martial. Let's assume he went to court-martial and was acquitted. If that were the end of it, that would be okay. But the way the ICC is structured, you could have a three-judge ICC panel—including say one from Libya and one from Syria—decide that the U.S. military justice system doesn't meet international standards and therefore we want to haul this soldier in front of the International Criminal Court, and they could do it."

Ralston said, "When I talked to my military colleagues when the treaty was being written in Rome, the first shocking thing was nobody was even aware this was being done. And when I explained it to them, they were horrified. In the U.S., the military is involved in these decisions. We can bring issues of concern to the political leadership, and in the other countries that's not true."

I told General Ralston that it was simply amazing that the Europeans don't require their senior military officers to give their best advice to all parliamentary decision makers. He said, "They don't—with some exceptions. It was absolutely stunning to me that they didn't. And part of that is because of the parliamentary system. Their minister of defense is [a member of Parliament]," and, Ralston implied, doesn't want the military leaders talking to the opposition.

Ralston said, "We have a very balanced system in America. The military is apolitical, which it has to be. But it also has to have hearings on the Hill. We swear, all of us at a senior level, sign a piece of paper that says if we're asked in a hearing on the Hill to give our personal view, even if it's in conflict with the administration we have to do it."

The military—contrary to the view of the American Left—is more often an important sanity check for politicians who might otherwise involve America in wars of choice, or fail to see wars of need. In the political buildup to the Iraq campaign of 2003, many retired generals and admirals—including Wesley Clark—testified in open House and Senate hearings about the Iraqi threat, and how any war should be conducted.

Of course, Europe has far different ideas about fighting terrorism, persisting in the belief, as Bill Clinton did, that it is a criminal rather than a war-fighting matter.

My friend Sir Timothy Garden, a retired Royal Air Force air marshal—now a well-respected defense author and commentator—told me that America shouldn't have taken any military action in response to the September 11, 2001, attacks, not even against Afghanistan's Taliban, who were providing a home base for al-Qaeda. Garden is not at all ignorant of America or its history. But he, like so many European intellectuals, sees a "more refined" approach as the better one. That "more refined" approach always involves the UN.

On June 3, 2003, French president Jacques Chirac said, "We consider that all military action not endorsed by the international community, through, in particular, the Security Council, was both illegitimate and illegal, is illegitimate and illegal. And we have not changed our view on that."[15] Many European leaders say the same. And many say worse.

Their deeply held view is that the American "hyperpower"—as they insist on calling us—is a great danger to the world. In December 2003, British military historian Corelli Barnett wrote to me:

You are of course correct in saying that the world's opinion of America does not alter the fact of hyperpowerdom. But when you claim that as a hyperpower you are entitled to "respect," you sound like nothing so much as the Kaiser's Germany demanding respect because it had the largest army and most powerful industrial machine in Europe. Rather than "respect," his Germany actually evoked awe and apprehension because of the coupling of its strength with the tone and thrust of its world policy. Leaving aside Washington's groupies like Blair and [Spanish former prime minister José María] Aznar, and Washington's clients like the Poles, this is broadly how Europeans (and, I suspect, Muslim states) regard Bush's America. "Respect" is what is accorded to good sense and wise leadership not to sheer power alone. "Appreciation" is what is accorded to generosity and public spirit, not to greed in consumption of the world's raw materials and energy supplies, nor to refusal to curb the world's single greatest output of environmental pollution. "Respect" and "admiration" (if you desire them) are to be earned, not merely expected as of right.

Hasn't America "earned" the respect of Europe over and over again, spending hundreds of thousands of lives to keep it free, and then asking little more than goodwill in return? Is America really to be feared, like the Kaiser's Germany was a century ago?

The subject of the Kaiser's Germany contains a valuable lesson about America, but not the one Professor Barnett states. In 1918, General John "Black Jack" Pershing was the commander of American forces in France. In May of that year, the Germans waged a large-scale attack that threw the French into disarray. The French demanded that the American forces be combined with theirs under French command. Pershing would have none of it. Eventually, the French sent a mission, under one Andre Tardeiu, to assess the U.S. forces. Tardeiu's report said it all:

The outstanding characteristics of Americans... are a highly developed national pride and a strong sense of independence.... They have decided not to submit to any subordination whatsoever, and have made up their minds to be placed on a footing of complete equality....

[W]e cannot flatter ourselves with the hope of forcing a complete and final adhesion to our way of thinking. The Americans are in the habit of listening to our views... but invariably reserve the right to make the final decision themselves, and are accustomed, in the last analysis, to base their decision on their own reasoning.[16]

Almost a century later France—and the UN—expected something different and uncharacteristic from America because they ignored our history and expected us to follow their lead. But America, unlike Old Europe, is not content to lie down and die.

The Ghosts of Old Europe

It is easy to relate Europe's anti-Americanism to jealousy of our wealth and power. Those elements are certainly part of the equation, but there are two additional factors buried much deeper in the European psyche. The burden of Europe's history is one, and the divergence of basic values is the other. Europe has drifted back to its 1930s view of dictators and despots. It will appease them as long as it can, and still rely on the United States to invest the money and blood it will take to defend it. Europe refuses to see two things.

First, Europe doesn't see that the threat of terrorism cannot be dealt with by containment, as the Soviets were. Terrorism threatens America and Europe with the same devastation—at any time—that America suffered on September 11, 2001, and that Spain suffered on March 11, 2004. French repression of its Muslim minority makes that threat more imminent.

Second, Europeans choose to ignore our mutual history with the ancestors of Muammar Qadafi: the first Islamic terrorists America encountered, the Barbary pirates. By 1804, and for at least a century before, the Barbary pirates—based in what are now Libya, Morocco, and Algeria—had been conducting a holy war against Western shipping. In this jihad, ships from Christian nations were routinely seized, their cargoes stolen, and their crews held for ransom. To protect their shipping in the Mediterranean (and not having an EU to do it for them) the Europeans were paying tribute—blackmail—to the pirate powers. France and Britain were paying the equivalent of hundreds of thousands of dollars a year in "protection" money to the pirates.[17] At first, the fledgling America chose to follow its European forbears with payment of tribute. But, as always, blackmail begat more blackmail. At that point, America made its historic choice and divided itself from Europe.

President Jefferson dispatched a small naval force, including a few U.S. Marines, to "chastise their insolence by sinking, burning, or destroying their ships and vessels wherever you shall find them," and to blockade Tripoli if it carried out its threat of war.[18] Jefferson's initiative was only partly successful because the force was inadequate to impose a regime change on the Barbary states. After the War of 1812, America formally declared war against Algiers, and sent ten ships under Stephen Decatur to finish the job. Decatur's ferocity in battle and victories in Algiers, Tunis, and Tripoli finally ended the threat of the Barbary pirates.

At the instant the new nation chose to spend its scarce funds on defense, and not on tribute, America molded a part of its character that has lasted to this day: to fight aggression, not appease it. By deciding on that course, America differentiated itself from its European forbears.

The EUnuchs now profess shock that America would act against Iraq instead of debate endlessly in the UN. If they cared to learn and apply the lessons of American history, they would know that is what America has always done in response to Middle Eastern threats. Two centuries ago, America built a fleet to "chastise" the Barbary pirates. In 1904, President Teddy Roosevelt sent another American fleet to rescue a single American citizen—Ion Perdicaris—who had been taken hostage by another Muslim bandit, the Moroccan Raisuli. Roosevelt's announced policy was "Perdicaris alive, or Raisuli dead." In 1990, when Saddam Hussein's Iraq invaded American ally Kuwait and threatened the oil fields of Saudi Arabia—both contrary to American interests—America sent an overwhelming force to repulse the Iraqis. Ignoring that history, the nearly three thousand dead on September 11, 2001, and the danger posed by Saddam's regime in Iraq, the Europeans are now shocked and angry that America wouldn't sit quietly and debate the issue of Iraq interminably in the UN.

Europe is outraged at American action in the Middle East because it refuses to realize that America hasn't fundamentally changed from the time Thomas Jefferson ordered the navy to fight the Tripolitan pirates. We have our historic model, and they have theirs, exemplified by Neville Chamberlain's appeasement of Hitler in the late 1930s.

We may not understand Europe as much as we might. But they understand us not at all and, for that, they have only themselves to blame.

CHAPTER ELEVEN

THE *EU*NUCHS AND THEIR UNION

*"There's a point, you know, where treachery is so complete
and unashamed that it becomes statesmanship."*

—George MacDonald Fraser[1]

SINCE 1950, THE MOVEMENT TOWARD A EUROPEAN UNION HAS DEVEL-
oped from a free-trade agreement to a more ambitious political union.[2]
In 2003, the European Union had fifteen members: Belgium, Denmark,
Germany, Greece, Spain, France, Ireland, Italy, Luxembourg, the Netherlands, Austria, Portugal, Finland, Sweden, and the United Kingdom. In
2004, it added ten more: the Czech Republic, Estonia, Cyprus, Latvia,
Lithuania, Hungary, Malta, Poland, Slovenia, and Slovakia.

The principal weakness of the EU is that its biggest members—
France and Germany—have decided it should be run as a Franco-
German alliance, and that other nations can join it only in a subordinate role. France and Germany make the rules, follow those they choose
to, and ignore the rest. About 50 percent of the EU's budget is spent
on agricultural subsidies that are—for the most part—paid to French

farmers. As Heritage Foundation expert Dr. John Hulsman put it, the agricultural subsidy is "really a sop from Germany to pay French farmers to sit around, play *boule*, and do nothing."

Our Enemy, France

Much of what France does is simply comical. Its insufferable affectations, its diplomatic arrogance, its government action to prevent English words from becoming part of the French language,[3] are all part of its desperate efforts to protect the nationalistic ego that William F. Buckley Jr. once declared France's greatest vulnerability. France's political culture is made up of equal parts conceit and greed. As British historian Paul Johnson told me, the "sheer malignity of France is one of the mysteries of history." Any perceived threat to French culture or identity is met with outrage bordering on hysteria. It's what Johnson called France's "cultural racism."

But each year, as its economy sinks and its posturing rises, France looks more and more like an aging whore piling on layer upon layer of makeup, desperate to conceal the truth. Aside from being a source of low comedy, France is a dedicated enemy of the United States.

In the unending UN Security Council debate about authorizing military action against Saddam Hussein, France was the leader of the opposition. An ally might have sat aside and refused to support America. But France chose to side with its client, Saddam Hussein, and did everything it could to stop the UN from acting to enforce its own resolutions. The result was black comedy. On January 30, 2003, I appeared on MSNBC's *Hardball with Chris Matthews*. When Matthews asked me whether we could go to war without the French, I said, "Frankly, going to war without France is like going deer hunting without an accordion. You just leave a lot of noisy, useless baggage behind."[4]

That got a lot of laughs, but it was quickly overshadowed by French actions so serious they could only be those of an enemy, not an errant ally. On March 28, 2003, ten days after Operation Iraqi Freedom began and Americans were fighting and dying in Iraq, France's foreign minister, Dominique de Villepin, was caught by reporters in London after giving a speech. As the *Daily Telegraph* reported it: "When asked: 'Who do you want to win the war?' de Villepin replied: 'I'm not going to answer. You have not been listening carefully to what I said before. You already have the answer.' " [5]

But he hadn't answered the question in his speech or anywhere else because, of course, he wanted Iraq to win. During the Iraq War, I hosted Oliver North's *Common Sense Radio* show while Ollie reported from the battlefield for FOX News Channel. When I mentioned de Villepin's comment on the air, the switchboard was flooded with calls from outraged Americans all across the country. Corelli Barnett more recently suggested we forgive de Villepin's arrogant remark because it was a "trick question." What is so tricky about it? Couldn't he at least have said, "Well, we wish the war had not been started, but of course we hope the Americans will succeed?" Of course he could have, but he didn't. As an experienced diplomat whose principal duty is to persuade the world to accept French policy and opinion, de Villepin spoke for the French government. As offensive and outrageous as his remark was, at least his reaction was honest. France wanted us to lose the Iraq War, and it did everything in its power to ensure that we did.

France was working against us even before the Iraq campaign. At that time still regarded as an American ally, it was receiving part of the intelligence information we gathered about Iraq, and passing this information right along to the Iraqis. As retired Air Force lieutenant general Thomas McInerney (now a senior military analyst for FOX News Channel), told me, "We know that the French government was passing along the intelligence information we shared with them to our enemies. They did this during the bombing campaigns in Kosovo and Belgrade, when they passed information to Milosevic. They passed intelligence information we gave them about Iraq straight through to Saddam Hussein. That's not the act of an ally. That's the act of an enemy." France has chosen to be our enemies' spy, and their arms merchant.

According to General McInerney, "We're now finding, among all the weapons Saddam's regime stockpiled in Iraq, many French weapons and other materials that France was apparently selling to the Iraqis in violation of the UN arms embargo. Included among them are Roland missiles, which are formidable weapons against aircraft and other targets."

What France does to oppose us militarily is matched perfectly to French actions that oppose us by intervening economically to help our enemies. France was the largest lender and contributor of funds to the regime of Saddam Hussein. And if you follow French money, you will find it in the hands of virtually every enemy America has and has had in the last four decades.

France is the number one lender to Cuba, Iran, Somalia, Sudan, and Vietnam.[6] French banks have lent about $2.5 billion to Iran alone.[7] U.S. banks are legally prohibited from lending money or investing in terrorist nations; French banks are not, and they seem to be everywhere American banks aren't.[8] The Communists used to say that capitalists would sell them the rope to hang them. France has a lot of rope to sell, and it would be pleased to see America dangling from it.

France's perpetuation of a Vichy foreign policy that cooperates with terrorists and dictators can be seen in its newest object of desire: Communist China, the fastest-growing major economy in the world. In January 2004, France lit up the Eiffel Tower in red to celebrate a visit by Chinese premier Hu Jintao. At the same time, France asked the EU to lift the ban on arms sales to China established after the Tiananmen Square massacre in 1989.[9] According to the French and Germans, China had made sufficient strides in improving human rights such that it no longer belonged in the same position as Myanmar (formerly Burma), Sudan, and Zimbabwe, the other nations to which arms sales are prohibited by the EU. Just what those improvements were was left unstated, for the principal reason that they are undetectable. The real reason for the French change of heart is its desire to benefit from China's huge defense budget.[10] The French will sell China anything it wants. And it wants a lot—to threaten Taiwan and extend its hege-mony all over the Pacific.

Mark Twain once said, "France has neither winter nor summer nor morals. Apart from these drawbacks, it is a fine country. France has usually been governed by prostitutes." *Plus ça change, plus c'est la même chose.*

France and the EU: *L'état C'est* Us

The EU has become France's tool in foreign policy. In its campaign to save its client, Saddam Hussein, France threatened Poland and other countries that their applications for EU admission would be denied if they sided with the United States. At an EU summit in February 2003, President Chirac described the behavior of the New Europe caste—Poland, Hungary, the Czech Republic, Latvia, Estonia, Lithuania, Slovenia, Slovakia, Romania, Bulgaria, Macedonia, Croatia, and Alba-nia—as "childish and dangerous." "They missed a good opportunity to keep silent," he said, referring to their signatures on two sets of statements demanding that Saddam Hussein comply with UN Security Council Resolution 1441. "These countries are very rude and rather reckless of the danger of aligning themselves too quickly with the Americans. Their situation is very delicate. If they wanted to diminish their chances of joining the EU, they couldn't have chosen a better way," he added, reminding these governments that a referendum in any one EU state could still block the entire enlargement process.[11]

Although France and Germany use the EU as a tool of their own pol-icy, they don't feel bound by its rules. The EU intends to combine its members' economies by making the euro its universal currency and coordinating the members' government spending and taxation rates. Germany insisted on—and won—limits on member states' deficits to 3 percent of their annual budgets. But Germany has violated its own rule, and so has France. In 2003, French debt exceeded the 3 percent GDP cap for the third year in a row. In fact, France and Germany are among the greatest government profligates. France's government outlays total more than 50 percent of its GDP.[12] Because France and Germany were susceptible to fines for breaking the debt cap, they bullied the EU into granting them an exemption in November 2003.[13]

Such shenanigans shouldn't surprise anyone—they're par for the course. For example, the French-led EUnuch bureaucrats find every way they can to compete with America, and they aren't hesitant to spend money to do it. Concerned by the success of FOX News Channel and many American television game shows in the European television markets, the EUnuchs came up with a way to compete. Not with better news coverage, of course.

In 2003, the EU paid about $2 million to establish a "school for soubrettes" which the *Daily Telegraph* described as teaching "young Italian women the not-so-subtle skills needed to become television game show hostesses and showgirls."[14] Apparently the EUnuchs, sitting in their ivory tower in Brussels, thought Italian women needed training in these skills. They should get out more. No one can complain about the expenditure, though, because the EU's own books— reflecting the bureaucracy's spending habits—don't balance sufficiently for outside auditors to state just how much is coming in, or going out, or even where it's going. They've had that problem for nine years running.[15]

But that's no reason for the EU parliament's members to take responsibility for the EU budget or deny themselves anything. On December 16, 2003, the European Commission angrily rejected a letter from the six richest members stating that the EU's budget should be limited to 1 percent of the total EU members' GNP. Two days later, the Euro-MPs voted themselves a 30 percent pay hike.[16] It doesn't take a crystal ball to see how the EU parliament will tax and spend to an excess that would make Ted Kennedy blush.

Still, in the long term, the EU, its euro, and the ambition to create a truly unified Europe could be in trouble. Swedish voters turned down the euro by a strong margin. Denmark and Estonia have rejected it.

British prime minister Tony Blair has resisted giving the British a vote on the question, but polls show that voters are opposed to it.

Under the EU's new constitution, which has yet to be ratified and might never be, member states will submit their national sovereignty—their economies and national defense—to the EU's government, its rotating presidency, its parliament, and the bureaucracy that thinks Italian women need training in how to flirt. This doesn't sound like a recipe for success.

The EU Constitution

Pomposity, thy name is Europe. The first declaration of the draft EU constitution begins with the words, "Conscious that Europe is a continent that has brought forth civilization...." Not *a* civilization—civilization. That claim is open to challenge by China, Egypt, and India, each of which had a head start by a few thousand years, more or less. And it goes on from there, at an equally grandiose level, for 265 pages, which include twenty-two pages of signatures, ruffles, flourishes, and self-congratulation.

Under the draft, member states agree:[17]

- To take no measure inconsistent with the objectives of the constitution (Art. 5, Sec. 2)
- To give a citizen of any EU country who happens to be resident in any other EU country voting rights and the right to run for local office (Art. 8, Sec. 2)
- That the EU constitution is superior to the laws of the individual member states, which includes treaties and other obligations (Art. 10)
- That the EU will govern their economic and employment policies (Art. 11, Sec. 3)
- That the EU will define and implement an EU foreign and security policy and develop a common defense policy (Art. 11, Sec. 4)

- That the EU will have the exclusive right to make international treaties on behalf of its members whenever such treaties involve matters of interest to the EU (Art. 12, Sec. 2)

Thus, under the EU constitution, member states surrender national sovereignty to the EU.[18]

The EU constitution has been years in the making, and was stopped dead in the water in December 2003 when an EU summit failed to reach agreement on the latest draft. Poland and Spain helped save the day for European nations that might want to escape the EU's overreach.

Three years before the December 2003 summit, in another EU summit held in Nice, Spain and Poland extracted concessions on representation in the EU parliament. Though France and Germany have about 60 percent of the EU's total population, Spain and Poland were much like the smaller states that demanded fair representation in the U.S. Congress at our constitutional convention in the 1780s. The EU draft constitution provides for "degressively" proportional representation, so Spain and Poland would have very little. When the 2003 summit met, they were under enormous pressure to give up what they had won in Nice, and they refused, which immediately led to recriminations, name-calling, and other usual Euro-diplomacy.

Indignant EU parliament member Klaus Haensch complained to the BBC. "Poland and Spain have shown that they are not at the level of European history," he said.[19] German chancellor Gerhard Schroeder called for a "two-speed" Europe: ratification of the draft constitution by those nations that were ready, and leaving the others behind. Jacques Chirac agreed. "I still think [the two-speed Europe] is a good solution. It would be a motor that would set an example. It will allow Europe to go faster, better."[20] Chirac is right. A two-speed Europe— one in the EU and one outside—would be very good. But only for those nations smart enough to stay out, grow their economies, and ensure their security, better and faster than the EU nations can, or will.

In Britain, Conservative Party leader Michael Howard sees value in the EU, so long as it is kept at arm's length. Howard told me, "My view is that Britain should not sign up to the constitution. I'm in favor of a different development altogether. I'm in favor of a much more flexible structure for the European Union under which those who wish to integrate more closely can do so, and those who don't—like the UK—while remaining a full member of the European Union are not obliged to sign up to any and every directive and regulation that emanates from Brussels...I believe that we should say to our partners that we have no desire to stop you from doing what you want to do as long as you don't make us do what we don't want to do."

Howard added, "There are some that would contend that we would continue to have authority over [defense, foreign, and tax policy] even if we signed up to the [EU] constitution.... I'm certainly against closer integration as far as Britain is concerned but I don't want to stop other states. If France and Germany want to do more things together, that's up to them." And so it should be. Those nations that wish to join the Franco-German alliance will make one choice, and those that do not will make a better one.

Spain, however, could backtrack. Shortly after the government of José Luis Rodríguez Zapatero was elected in Spain's March 2003 elections, he said he would concede the EU voting rights that had been won by the conservative government of José María Aznar. This left only Poland and Britain as serious opponents to the EU constitution. Both went wobbly all too quickly.

The Poles, lacking a strong economic position, are likely to cave. British prime minister Tony Blair has said that the UK should not sign the EU constitution unless it was changed to respect his "red line" issues: maintaining British independence on defense and foreign policy, taxation, social security, and the EU budget. In March 2004, Blair said that after the EU discussions fell apart in December 2003 an agreement to accommodate his concerns had been put in place.[21] The EUnuchs plan to propose another version later in 2004.

Conservative MP John Redwood—not one to mince words—told me on March 26, 2004, that, "Tony Blair will cave into Europe and agree to a constitution which will not be in Britain's interests and will not be supported by a majority of the British people. He is already giving ground over areas of criminal justice that the EU will be able to run rather than the UK Parliament, just as he is giving away the UK's right to an independent asylum and borders policy." Redwood and Howard may get a fair crack at the EU constitution. In late April 2004, Prime Minister Blair announced that a referendum on the EU constitution would be held, and the citizens of the UK allowed to decide for themselves. It's a very risky move for Blair, and could result in the fall of his government.

The Brits might yet save themselves from the EU constitution. If they do, they will give strength to other would-be opponents of the Franco-German alliance that may drag all of continental Europe down the same socialist economic drain, and into their Potemkin military.

CHAPTER TWELVE

NATO AND THE *EU*NUCH MILITARY

"I hope that I shall never see the day when the Force of Right is deprived of the Right of Force."

—Winston Churchill

ADAM SMITH MUST BE LOOKING DOWN FROM HEAVEN AND SIGHING IN disgust at the nations of Old Europe. Not only are they uniting on terms that violate every economic principle he pronounced in *The Wealth of Nations*, they are ignoring their principal duty to their people. As Smith wrote:

> The first duty of the sovereign, therefore, that of defending the society from the violence and injustice of other independent societies, grows gradually more and more expensive as the society advances in civilization. The military force of the society...must, in the progress of improvement, first be maintained by him in time of war, and afterwards even in time of peace.[1]

This expense must be borne, Smith wrote, because "defense is more important than opulence." That, too, is rejected in the founding principles of the EU. There is no statement of the duty to provide adequately for defense. The EUnuchs, having disarmed themselves, are now combining their weak militaries into what they say will be a powerful military force. But the whole will be considerably less than the sum of its parts.

Since the fall of the Soviet Empire, almost all of the European nations have failed to devote any significant part of their national budgets to building and maintaining their armed forces. The United States usually devotes about 3 to 3.5 percent of our GDP to defense spending. In Europe, only Britain and France spend a like percentage. The rest—like Germany, which spends about 1 percent of its GDP on defense, and Italy, which spends about 0.9 percent—simply refuse to invest in defense at an adult level.

In short, the EUnuchs have disarmed to the point that they couldn't defend themselves. Despite everything they do to thwart American policy, they still expect that we will defend them.

As Dr. John Hulsman told me, "When I started my career, three countries in NATO spent legitimate amounts, say 2.5 percent [of GDP] and above, on defense. They were France, Britain, and the United States. At this stage of my career, three countries spend legitimate amounts of money—France, Britain, and the United States. When I'm dead, the same countries will spend the same amount. There is no movement toward significant increases in defense spending to pass the laugh test. I mean to be taken seriously as a military force that is deployable, modern, and can be anywhere in the world."

Although they lack the capability to defend themselves, the EU nations nevertheless want to establish their independence from American defense. The EU constitution requires the member nations to join together in a common defense policy that will be conducted by the EU government. One problem for the United States is that the EU constitution preempts all preexisting treaties, implicitly including the NATO mutual defense treaty with the United States. The EU defense structure is being postured as one independent from NATO.

Europe needs to unlearn some of the lessons it wants to pass along to us. We are told that it took Europe two horrendous wars to give up on military solutions to their disputes. That is nonsense, because it ignores external threats and doesn't even consider internal ones. It took American military action—at great cost in blood and treasure—to save Europe from itself, twice. It cost us far more in money (and thankfully much less in blood) to face down and defeat the Soviet Union. In response, Europe has taken a childish and irresponsible attitude toward its own defense. It has literally given up.

For Germany to be spending about 1 percent of its GDP on defense presumes two things: first, that there is no significant threat to Germany; and second, that if such a threat arose, others would defend Germany. The same is true for the other defaulters on defense spending. Spain, Italy, and so many others fail in their principal duty to their citizens: to provide for their defense.

The first assumption may seem craven, but is merely pragmatic. Europe and America vie for commercial advantage throughout most of the world. In the Far East, American power protects American interests and European interests indivisibly. If America were a colonial power—as many Europeans see us—we would be seizing those markets by force and impeding European trade. In reality, the EU gets a free ride because when we keep the oceans and skies free for foreign trade, we do so without limiting who can take advantage of that freedom.

Europeans believed—at least until the March 2004 Madrid train bombings—that terrorist threats to America were not pointed at Europe. Bin Laden declared war on America, not Europe. Communist China—at least a regional threat to American interests in the Far East—is not seen as a threat to Europe. America, not Europe, is committed to defend Taiwan if China attacks.

There is—so far—only one mutual threat that some in Europe perceive and are willing to face: the proliferation of missiles and nuclear weapons to despots and terrorists. North Korea—a radical and uncontrolled proliferator of missiles and nuclear technology—is the principal target of the Proliferation Security Initiative, which requires military action against international commerce in weapons.

But here's the rub. Among the eleven members of the PSI—Australia, France, Germany, Italy, Japan, the Netherlands, Poland, Portugal, Spain, the United Kingdom, and the United States—only the UK, Australia, the U.S., and France have credible forces that can engage in the global effort required. The others are limited to regional efforts and aren't planning to build the forces necessary to fully contribute to their own defense against weapons of mass destruction.

Paper Tiger

In November 2002, while the EU constitution was still in the early drafting stages, France and Germany proposed a "full European security and defense union" with an "integrated command capability" armed by a "European Armaments Agency."[2] The French and Germans wanted a unified system of military training and a shared strategic doctrine.[3] The British strongly resisted the idea, wanting to keep NATO together without having the EU split from it like France did in the 1960s. The principal reasons for the EU's drive for defense independence are commercial: to sell European arms to the European Armaments Agency and to shut out American arms companies from Europe.

On January 18, 2004, General Gustav Hagglund, chairman of the EU military committee, said that Europe should defend itself and split NATO:

> The American and European pillars [of NATO] would be responsible for their respective territorial defenses, and would together engage in crisis management outside their

own territories...My prediction is that this will happen in the next decade.[4]

Hagglund added, "We don't know if the United States will have forever the resources or the interest, to defend Europe."[5] But will Europe have the resources to defend itself?

Back in June 2001, eleven distinguished British and French generals and admirals sent a remarkable letter to the *Daily Telegraph* newspaper. Their warning exposes the dangers of European defense that the EU nations—at least France and Germany—so eagerly seek to bring on themselves:

> While close cooperation should quite rightly take place, common cause does not mean that we should dilute our forces in a common army, navy or air force. As former servicemen, we wish to voice our concerns at the manner in which the ability of our nations to protect our vital interests is being whittled away.
>
> First, by penny-pinching, cutbacks in procurement and in force strength. Second, by overstretch, committing reduced forces to increased global peacekeeping commitments, with disastrous effects on retention and morale. Third, and most important, by forging a common pseudo-identity in EU defence and foreign policy.
>
> Our two countries have differing views on the future role and shape of NATO. But we can build on our distinctiveness if our armed forces remain under national flags. A common Euro army is incompatible with both of our approaches to this issue.
>
> The actions of federalist politicians and technocrats playing at armchair generals, building a fictitious paper army, will only serve to weaken even further our national

capabilities to the detriment of our own security and world stability. They should be aware: paper tigers burn.

For the sake of our two countries and for Europe as a whole, we would counsel throwing the scheme into the dustbin of history before the fires begin.[6]

What the generals and admirals said was that the EU emperor was naked, without the armor he needs to protect himself. The reduced defense expenditures and the casual use of their nation's forces on UN peacekeeping missions (where their nation's interests might not be implicated) reduce their forces to a dangerously weak level. As the admirals and generals reminded the EU, paper tigers burn. The EU members should think about what might happen if the ill-regarded American "hyperpower" sends marshmallows instead of Marines to the fire.

Reforming NATO

If the EU intends to compete with NATO, and if many NATO nations are practically disarmed, is NATO worth saving? The answer is "yes," but the alliance needs to be reformed.

NATO was founded because the nations of the West were held together by what Air Chief Marshall Sir Brian Burridge called "the glue of fear" regarding the aggressive intentions of the Soviet Union.[7] Under Article 5 of the NATO charter, all of the member nations pledged to come to the defense of any other that was attacked. Only once in NATO's history was Article 5 invoked, in response to the September 11, 2001, attacks on America.

Alliances fail for one of three reasons. Some fail to act when called upon, as SEATO—the Southeast Asian Treaty Organization—did when its members declined to help America in Vietnam. Others fail when the nations that belong to them undergo fundamental change, as did CENTO (the Central Treaty Organization in the Middle East) when Iran fell to the mullahs. The last reason they fail is that the interests of nations change, and with that change necessarily comes the reordering of alliances.

The Atlantic Alliance is being challenged from within by the EU separating its defense policy from that of the United States. Fortunately, Britain (or at least British conservatives) opposes the separation. Prime Minister Tony Blair, of the Labour Party, has often said that he would not put NATO at risk, but has sent mixed signals over the French and German proposal to set up a separate NATO command structure.

Some of the damage to NATO results from Old Europe's action in the UN, and those wounds (at least between America, France, and Germany) are far from healed. But some of the damage has been done—unintentionally—by America.

General Joe Ralston began his term as supreme allied commander, Europe, in 2000. Ralston served in that post after having been both head of U.S. European command and vice chairman of the Joint Chiefs of Staff. He told me how the damage to NATO occurred, and how it was repaired.

General Ralston said, "There was a lot of angst in the spring of 2001 because Condi Rice said, during the election campaign, if George Bush is elected president, we're pulling out of Bosnia. We're getting out of the Balkans. And that caused a lot of nervousness. Then, shortly after the election, Secretary Rumsfeld made a comment similar to that. Secretary Powell had to pour some oil on the waters and he got everything calmed down again. Then President Bush came over on the thirteenth of June, and there was a heads of state meeting in Brussels. The president did a very good job of getting people calmed down again. But they'd gone through a very uneasy springtime.

"Then September comes along, and 9-11 hits. And the nations really wanted to help because they thought America might withdraw from the alliance. We had all the comments about the mission should determine the coalition, not the other way around and all of that and it had an unsettling effect on the alliance."

Sir Timothy Garden said that American reaction to the September 11, 2001, attacks damaged NATO again. When NATO invoked Article 5 of its charter, calling for mutual defense of the United States, the Bush administration's initial reaction was, according to Garden, a dismissive "don't call us, we'll call you." General Ralston said that was a fair characterization. But things changed rapidly, and NATO—with the exception of France—helped considerably in Afghanistan and also in the buildup to the Iraq campaign. NATO—according to Ralston—still works.

General Ralston said, "There's more good going on in NATO than they're getting credit for. If we go back to last February [2003], the United States asked NATO for three things. They asked for NATO AWACS [airborne warning and control systems aircraft] over Turkey, Patriot missiles to protect Turkish cities from potential retaliation by Iraqi Scud missiles, and for ships of the alliance to provide escort duties through the Straits of Gibraltar and the entryway to the Suez Canal. NATO had a debate for eleven days. After that debate, all eighteen members of the integrated military structure voted to do exactly what the United States asked.... It was not fair to characterize NATO as totally fractured, unable to make a decision, can't do anything right. There was a split between France and the eighteen members of the integrated military structure but even Belgium—when it got down to it—said this is the right thing to do and we're going to do it."

Is the damage to NATO reparable? Ralston said it not only was, but that the repair has already been accomplished. As he explained it, welcoming NATO into Afghanistan and Iraq helped enormously. "They very much want the United States to be a part of the alliance and take advantage of it." And so we must.

America, rich and powerful though it is, should not have to fight the war against terror by itself. As Paul Wolfowitz told me, "I really think that the foundation of our security for the last fifty years, and even more so for the next hundred, does come from alliance with countries that share our values. If we had to do it by ourselves, it would be much more difficult. In fact, literally by ourselves, it would be impossible."

Wolfowitz's thinking is consistent with that of key British conservatives. Conservative Party leader Michael Howard told me, "One of the things that I regard as absolutely of huge importance in managing the problems that the world faces is the preservation and promotion of partnership between Europe and the United States. If Europe and the United States become rivals rather than partners, I think all the dangers the world faces will be much worse and much greater to overcome... huge efforts need to be made to manage any disagreements which occur, in a way that does as little damage as possible to the promotion of this partnership. Because if we wake up one morning and find that it's no longer there, the world's going to be a much more difficult place to live in."

Test Case: Spain

Unfortunately, the March 11, 2004, Madrid train bombings, which are being called "3-11" in Europe, might indicate that the Europeans will try to appease radical Islamic terror rather than work with the United States to fight it.

For al-Qaeda, bombing Spain was a brilliant tactical choice. Because the Muslims occupied most of Spain for centuries, any reassertion of Islamic power there has enormous significance to the Arab world. Moreover, before the March elections, Spanish prime minister José María Aznar had been one of America's staunchest allies. At the time of the election, about 1,300 Spanish troops were among the coalition forces in Iraq. During the election campaign, Aznar's principal opponent—socialist José Luis Rodríguez Zapatero—promised to withdraw Spanish troops from Iraq and weaken the Spanish alliance with America. Spain—obviously vulnerable to terrorist attack—was picked for a terrorist-forced regime change.

Just four days before the election, on March 11, 2004, ten bombs exploded on trains and in stations along a commuter rail line to Madrid, Spain. At least two hundred people were killed and more than 1,200 injured.[8] Aznar's government at first reflexively blamed the Basque terrorist group ETA. But from the start, there were reports of anomalies in these bombings. ETA usually gives warning of attacks, and it typically uses different kinds of explosives and detonators than were used that day. When night fell on March 11, intelligence and military experts were raising the possibility of Islamist terror. Soon an organization related to al-Qaeda—the Abu Hafs al-Masri Brigade—claimed responsibility for the bombings.

Three days later, on the eve of the Spanish elections, al-Qaeda obliged the Spaniards with a message claiming it was responsible for the attacks. It said:

> We declare our responsibility for what happened in Madrid exactly 2.5 years after the attacks on New York and Washington. It is a response to your collaboration with the criminals Bush and his allies.
>
> This is a response to the crimes that you have caused in the world, and specifically in Iraq and Afghanistan, and there will be more, if God wills it.
>
> You love life and we love death, which gives an example of what the Prophet Mohammad said. If you don't stop your injustices, more and more blood will flow and these attacks will seem very small compared to what can occur in what you call terrorism.
>
> This is a statement by the military spokesman for al-Queda in Europe, Abu Dujan al Afghani.[9]

It was a masterful move by al-Qaeda, and it worked. The Spanish, a proud and strong people, collapsed like a house of cards. In an unusually high voter turnout, Aznar's government was defeated and replaced by the socialist appeaser, Zapatero. Spain's election of Zapatero will boost al-Qaeda recruitment for years to come. Unless we destroy the terrorists first.

Before the Spanish election, the regime change scorecard favored the West: two to none. Iraq and Afghanistan were on the side of the West as victories against terrorist sponsors. With Zapatero's victory in the election, the score became two to one. We cannot win this war at that rate.

Zapatero was quick to hand al-Qaeda the fruits of its strategic victory. He reinforced the Islamist belief that the West was corrupt, decadent, and cowardly. And the ever-appeasing EUnuchs quickly joined in Zapatero's declaration of surrender.

European Commission president Romano Prodi told the press that, "It is clear that using force is not the answer to resolving the conflict with terrorists. We must remember that it has been a year since the war in Iraq started. Terrorism is infinitely more powerful than a year ago."[10]

If Osama bin Laden had drafted Prodi's talking points, they could not have been better written to strengthen the terrorists' hand. Al-Qaeda had not had any major successes between September 11, 2001, and March 11, 2004. Its resources, its people, and its international network had been substantially weakened by the efforts of the American-led coalition. Now, with a successful attack on a key coalition member, both that nation and the rest of the EUnuchs were ready to concede to fear and failure.

Having succeeded in Spain, terrorists now see an opportunity to topple their principal enemy, George W. Bush. If Bush is defeated and John Kerry succeeds him, America might well revert to Clintonism, its feckless law-enforcement approach to fighting terror, and its surrender of American foreign policy to the United Nations.

America's Responsibility: To Lead

Despite the EU's machinations and pretensions to global power, there is no reason for America to reject Europe the same way we should reject the UN. NATO remains a vital transatlantic link on which to build.

The structure of NATO, and the familiarity one nation's military has with the others, is a tremendous asset that cannot be recreated on a whim. Though politicians maneuver for power and change, most of the NATO nations' militaries maneuver—train, equip, and operate—with each other. And in doing so, they make each other stronger. No matter how well America's military can fight alone, it can do so better with the allies it knows, and it knows the NATO forces almost as well as it knows itself. NATO should be led into the twenty-first century by American cooperation, leadership, and above all, vision.

For more than half a century, NATO has been the face of Western power. In politics, as in sales, brand names have value. NATO is a powerful brand name in global affairs that cannot be allowed to dissolve because some of its members lack the courage and the foresight to believe that the West needs to remain united. To save NATO, action has to be taken on both the military and political fronts.

Sir Brian Burridge said that most European nations realize that NATO cannot be just a political alliance; it must have a credible military underpinning. "NATO has been held together by the military more than by the politicians, and it must continue to be so. The military cooperates in ways politicians can't." In the military aspect of reforming NATO, we have to begin with what NATO can do, and must be able to do in the future.

General Ralston sees it this way. "We have to go back to what is the mission of NATO. In my view, NATO's mission is to provide for stability and security in the NATO area of responsibility. There are times when NATO needs to operate outside their traditional area of responsibility.... But for years and years there has been a theological argument whether NATO could operate out of area. If nothing else, 9-11 solved that problem because it was dramatic evidence that a threat to a nation's security doesn't have to come from its immediate adjacent neighbor. You have to fall back and ask what are the most likely threats to the security of those nations and what kind of forces do you need to meet that threat."

NATO's longstanding linkage of America and Western Europe's militaries is its principal asset: It's called "muscle memory." It starts with the individual soldier.

Major Roger Carstens is the company commander of the Special Forces Qualification Course at the U.S. Army's Special Forces School at Fort Bragg, North Carolina. Carstens has the responsibility to ensure that young soldiers, who are already highly trained, are molded into some of the most capable special operations troops in the world. A basic foundation of their skills is "muscle memory." As Carstens describes it:

> Motor skills—such as shooting—are trained by repetition, creating a "muscle memory" that repeats the action instinctively, letting the soldier think about fighting rather than being distracted by the steps of, say, reloading his weapon. On a larger scale, by repeatedly conducting mission-essential tasks under the stress of a simulated combat environment, we can reduce the friction and confusion that occurs in battle. Here at the U.S. Army Special Warfare School we conduct "battle drills," in which units conduct actions in contact with a simulated enemy. This creates a sort of "muscle memory" at the individual and unit level, implanting a nearly instinctive feel for each other's movements on the battlefield. Nowhere has this proved more valuable than at the Joint Operational level, where repetitive training and habitual relationships facilitate the conduct of complex combat exercises.

What begins with the soldier continues up in the military chain to units, joint commands, and alliances such as NATO. NATO's "muscle memory" was developed in fifty years of joint training and war gaming, joint strategy and tactics development, and exchange programs. During the Cold War, American officers went to NATO nations' military schools in exchange programs, and those nations sent their college-age would-be officers to America's military academies. Active units from America's services trained continuously with NATO forces, and conducted military exercises all over the NATO theaters. In the elaborate American military exercises here in the U.S., it was a rare occasion that forces from one or more NATO members weren't participating.

But because the Europeans invest too little in defense—especially since the end of the Cold War—"muscle memory" is being lost. When the European members of NATO joined in the 1991 Gulf War, they found themselves at least a generation behind American military technology. Major General Burt Moore was director of operations for U.S. Central Command, the principal organizer of the war for General Norman Schwarzkopf.

Moore told me that the nations that came to the war varied enormously in their capability. "Among the top forces, aside from the U.S., the Brits were top-notch in their ground and air forces, and their special forces. After that, it drops off fairly dramatically."[11] The real key is the ability—which means having compatible technology—to train and fight alongside American forces. In the military, they call this "interoperability." Moore said, "If you talk about interoperability and compatibility it was a very serious problem. . . . Of course, because of the British involvement with NATO forces, we had less problem with them."

NATO is still more capable—and has more "muscle memory"—than any other military alliance. How long that will last depends on how many of the NATO nations can make themselves able to "plug and play."

"Plug and play" warfare—also called "network-centric" warfare—is the military label for the complex technological and organizational linkage that has been developed in American forces. Retired Air Force lieutenant general Thomas McInerney defines network-centric warfare this way:

> [N]etwork-centric warfare is the strategic combination of all forces—air, land, sea, and space—in the way they can best operate jointly. A network-centric joint force is the flesh on a skeleton of technology that provides information and data from every level to every level and gives top commanders the ability to delegate more decisions to lower levels, adding

considerably to tactical flexibility and effectiveness. It also minimizes the time consumed by decision makers, making it far less than the comparable effort takes in the enemy's headquarters. We can thus get inside the enemy's decision cycle, which is essential for victory in modern fast-moving warfare.

By the time the 1991 Gulf War began, the Pentagon had been investing in and designing a war network for almost a decade. When our allies showed up, many were sidelined because they couldn't operate within the network of war. After that war, many Europeans learned the wrong lesson. Instead of trying to modernize, they simply gave up. By the 2003 Iraq campaign, American forces were so tightly linked by technology that any forces that weren't both equipped and trained for the network-centric war were of little value.

Sir Brian Burridge said, "We live in an era of 'plug and play' warfare. You're either part of the network, or you're not relevant. To be part of it, you have to invest both money and thought in the compatibility 'umbrella'—the overall strategic and tactical structure of computer networks, weapon systems, and people that make the forces able to 'plug and play.'" By 2004, according to both Burridge and Moore, most of the NATO nations are at least one generation behind America, and in some cases—such as Germany, Belgium, and the Netherlands—they are at least two generations behind.

With their irresponsible approach to defense, the other NATO nations will never catch up to American military technology. As Burt Moore put it, "When you say a ten-year program, if the Germans for example are going to stay at 1 percent of GDP spending on defense, how about a hundred-year program?"

Specialization and Refinement of Tasks

One possible solution is for military specialization among some of the NATO nations. Some, like the UK and the U.S., can aim to do everything. Others, like the Netherlands, can focus on a single poten-tial strength to bring to the modern battlefield. General Ralston said, "We have always had specialization. The idea that Latvia is going to be a mirror image of the United States military is just ridiculous."

NATO could, as Ralston envisions, become a "modularized" mili-tary, with Latvia, for example, becoming the NATO component responsible for mine clearing; Poland's very capable special forces focusing on bridge-taking; and so on. But there are two problems with that approach. First is that in order to do it, NATO's members would first still have to become baseline network-centric and compatible with American capabilities, which means an enormous European investment in technology and people.

The second problem is that if America didn't reduce or eliminate its own capabilities in these specialized areas, it would be a powerful deterrent to the European states to take specialization seriously, and to invest in it. Though there are shortfalls—such as cargo airlift and sealift, as well as airborne tankers to refuel long-range aircraft—Ameri-can forces have every capability they need to fight anywhere at any time. To become dependent on others for even small specializations is a mistake. But if modular reform becomes the model, some compro-mises with trusted allies might have to be considered.

Burridge has another model for reforming NATO. "One way for NATO to revitalize itself is to focus it on providing homeland defense for all its members," Burridge said. "Reuniting NATO's military around [a new common air defense] capability would bring some of the less-involved nations back into the fold. Some of the Baltic States, for example, are new NATO members, and have no indigenous air defense. By joining with NATO to provide it, they can be better integrated into both the mutual commitments of NATO nations, and the NATO force structure." In Burridge's view, the consolidation of defenses such as these is something that all NATO nations have a vested interest in accomplishing.

While Ralston and Burridge pose valid theories for reforming NATO, both fail for the same reason: politics. The political climate within most NATO members precludes spending enough on defense to transform their militaries into network-centric forces.

Europe looks at defense spending as a kind of corporate social welfare. Europe is now investing its few precious defense euros on weapon systems that are taking it backward, not forward. According to General Ralston, "The two poster children for that are the A400-M and Galileo. The A400-M is a large transport aircraft.... Even on paper, it's inferior to two airplanes that are in existence today that happen to be made by the United States: the C-17 and the C-130. But, for political reasons, they are going to go forward ... with the A400-M. They'll spend billions of dollars to design this airplane."

Ralston's point is well taken. The Europeans will spend less, and they will spend it in the worst way: building assets that are obsolete or redundant. "Galileo is an even more egregious example," Ralston said. "Here, you're going to spend billions and billions of euros and put up a cheap GPS [global positioning system] which you'll charge people to use, when GPS is already up there, free for everyone." And the EUnuchs are doing it only to subsidize their own defense industries.

The Europeans will not develop serious militaries until they conclude that radical Islamic terrorism is a threat to them and merits a military response, and that defense spending is as important as socialist welfare spending. Neither has happened, nor is it likely to. If a hijacked airliner knocked down the Eiffel Tower, France would find a way to blame the United States and Israel.

Reforming NATO cannot begin in that political environment. So it is up to the United States to change the political environment by telling the Europeans that America's defense guarantee is over. The new NATO must be a true alliance of states that share similar values, strategic interests, and military capabilities, not a military welfare program for Europe.

Three Principles for a New NATO

Spite and revenge are poor foundations for policy. It would be quite easy, and profoundly wrong, to say that the nations participating in the UN defeats on Iraq can no longer be our allies. It would be just as easy—and just as wrong—to say that NATO would be better off without any of those nations. NATO's membership must be changed, but not because of a few UN votes. A new NATO must be structured on the basis of shared values, strategies, and capabilities, as well as acceptance of the necessity of mutual defense. And it is precisely on those bases that some nations—beginning with France and Germany—can no longer be America's defense partners in NATO.

There is no reason to threaten the EU with the dissolution of NATO. Threats of withdrawing American defense from nations signing the EU constitution would only increase anxiety over the hegemonic intent of the American "hyperpower" and work against American interests. America should be reforming NATO along the lines it is using to draw nations away from the UN. NATO should be reformed into an alliance in which membership would be a privilege instead of something owed to those who merely occupy a particular geographic space.

That France cannot be America's partner was not proved in the UN, but on the ground in Iraq. Germany's political fealty to France and the EU can be forgiven. Its unilateral disarmament cannot. Those other nations of NATO that choose France or Germany's path cannot be our allies. NATO needs to evolve from within, in accordance with three principles.

First, America should only obligate itself to mutual defense of those nations that share its national security objectives in the post-Soviet era. Defending France conflicts with that principle, so France must be excluded from NATO. Second, America must only agree to mutual defense of those nations that are investing—in proportion to their size and wealth—in their own defense. Germany, and others which have unilaterally disarmed, cannot participate in mutual defense. Third, there are some nations—in NATO and elsewhere—that America must agree to defend even if they do not defend themselves because they are strategically located and share America's objectives.

To accomplish NATO reform under those principles, it is necessary to reform it from within, gradually changing its internal structure. Intelligence, military technology, strategy, and tactics we must reserve for ourselves and our real allies. Another step we have to take is to withdraw American forces from nations such as Germany where they serve no useful purpose. This is not punishment for German perfidy in the UN. It is part of the reformation of NATO as well as the recognition that we must use our limited forces more effectively.

Those NATO members that, like Germany, fail to spend sufficiently to defend themselves should lose their privileges of participating in American training and planning. The Germans, who have a major Luftwaffe flight training center at Holloman Air Force Base, New Mexico, should be told to pack up and go home. And when we tell them to go, we should explain it in terms of Germany's utter failure to keep up its part of the NATO bargain. It isn't spending sufficiently on defense to maintain its obligations, so we must choose not to do it for them. Other nations that have forces here, even temporarily, should be asked to leave if they are failing to invest in their own defense, and are utterly unable to participate in network-centric warfare. Should those conditions change, and those nations again undertake their own defense, they should be invited back to train in America, and into the center of NATO.

NATO now functions through several committees. The principal one, the Defense Planning Committee, already excludes France because of its pullout from the NATO military structure in the 1960s. Other member states that do not adequately maintain their militaries to a "plug and play" standard should also be excluded from the committee (which is for ministers at the level of the secretary of defense in America), but be allowed to keep their seats on the Defense Review

Committee, which serves a lesser advisory function. Simultaneously, the United States should take the lead in drawing up a new NATO charter for the twenty-first century that will exclude nations that do not share a similar political and strategic vision and similar rates of defense expenditure with the United States. The new NATO will be better suited to mutually beneficial consultation, cooperation, and action.

As British Conservative Party leader Michael Howard told me, "[T]here are things which need to be done on both sides of the Atlantic. A lot of the criticisms of the United States for unilateral action are misplaced. The United States has attempted to consult very often before it has taken action. The impression is different from the reality, and I would like to see . . . greater attempts to be made for the United States to be seen to be consulting with its European partners before decisions are made. Obviously there won't always be unanimity and nobody's suggesting that the ability of the United States to act should be constrained. But it would be helpful, I think, to overcome what are frequently false impressions of American unilateralism if more—and more obvious and conspicuous—consultation took place."

We need to transform NATO gradually back to what it was: the principal military alliance of the West, ready to meet the new century's threats.

CHAPTER THIRTEEN

FORWARD TOGETHER, OR NOT

"The choice is in our own hands, like the Israelites of old, blessing and cursing is not before us. Today we can have the greatest failure or the greatest triumph—as we choose. There is enough for all. The earth is a generous mother. Never, never did science offer such fairy gifts to man. Never did their knowledge and science stand so high. Repair the waste. Rebuild the ruins. Heal the wounds. Crown the victors. Comfort the broken and broken-hearted. There is the battle we have won to fight. There is the victory we have now to win. Let us go forward together."

—Winston Churchill, 1917

THE BANNER ON THE UNITED NATION'S WEBSITE PROCLAIMS, "WEL-come to the UN. It's Your World." But it's not our world, the one that defends freedom and opposes oppression. More often, the United Nations opposes freedom and defends terrorism and tyranny. It reflects its membership, which reflects the world, where most countries are nei-ther democracies nor wedded to Western ideas of individual liberties and rights.

Winston Churchill spoke of the United Nations in his "Iron Curtain" speech of March 5, 1945, saying, "We must make sure that its work is fruitful, that it is a reality and not a sham, that it is a force for action, and not merely a frothing of words, that it is a true temple of peace in which the shields of many nations can some day be hung up, and not merely a cockpit in a Tower of Babel."

But the UN has become precisely what Churchill hoped it would not be: a Tower of Babel—and we pay for it. Most important, we pay for it politically, because the United Nations has become a tool for spreading anti-American ideas around the world.

Amazingly, the EU—the Europe that America has rescued in two world wars at immense cost—has also turned against us. The countries of Old Europe—and France in particular, because of its veto in the Security Council—are the most effective allies of the rogue nations, corrupt bureaucrats, and Third World failures of the United Nations. The UN and Old Europe are united in seeing America as a threat to their own powers. France, as the leader of Old Europe, believes it must challenge American action on virtually every economic, diplomatic, and military front in order to support its claim to be a global power, just as the UN must challenge us to maintain the façade of being the arbiter of world affairs. Many states within the EU follow France's lead and see their role as competing against America, rather than cooperating with us.

This is why far worse than the UN's annual $7 billion economic cost to the United States is its political cost. The UN gives the illusion of legitimacy to causes and political positions that don't deserve it, and allows our self-appointed rivals in Old Europe to pose as speaking for the world, and not merely for their own narrow interests. The United Nations and Old Europe collect our money and sometimes pose as our friends, but America gets nothing out of the deal, except abuse.

A division of interests between the United States and Europe after the Cold War was inevitable, but the eight years of the Clinton administration—which gave the United Nations control over American foreign policy and national security—accelerated the division of the West by increasing the authority of the UN at America's expense, and by convincing France and the UN Security Council that they could dictate American foreign policy.

Though Bill Clinton and his liberal predecessor Jimmy Carter deserve enormous blame for accelerating this division of the West and endangering America, their actions are in the past. America is about to choose its future. The American people face an election in November 2004 as dramatic as the Spanish faced in March 2004—but with much, much higher stakes. President George W. Bush puts America's interests first and believes in taking action when action is necessary for America's security. His challenger, John F. Kerry, would return us to the days of Clinton, put American foreign policy at the mercy of the United Nations, and give the French a veto on American military action.

As Senator Kerry said on *Meet the Press* on April 18, 2004, he believes that the war on terror "is not primarily a military operation. It's an intelligence gathering, law enforcement, public diplomacy effort, and we're putting far more money into the war on the battlefield than we are into the war of ideas." He promised that, within weeks of being inaugurated, he would personally go to the UN and "literally, formally rejoin the community of nations." In short, Kerry will repeat the foreign policy of Bill Clinton, and fail in just the same way.

The Way Forward

That the UN has failed in performing as a forum to resolve the world's conflicts peacefully does not condemn us to eternal war. That some members of NATO value competition over cooperation is a natural evolution of nations' interests that does not prevent NATO from being reformed and rebuilt. That America was unable to gather France and Germany into its coalition of the willing (of forty-eight other nations) to free Iraq does not mean that America has failed itself or the world.

It is important for America to build new alliances geared to the war we're in now—as President Bush has done with Kyrgyzstan and Uzbekistan, and with tremendous effect in India. As Paul Wolfowitz explained to me, "[O]ne of the important issues that this president is already mastering is to strengthen this relationship with democratic India. It started before September 11, and it's been paying dividends even before September 11."

Wolfowitz told me, "[T]he most important dividend is one we didn't anticipate.... It was to help India manage its relationship with Pakistan so that Pakistan could be extremely helpful to us in Afghanistan. If you stop and think about what might have happened if the crisis between [India and Pakistan resulted in a war] and even if it didn't go nuclear, what would have happened to our position in Afghanistan? It would have been crippling. The fact that we were able to have influence and they didn't have that war was enormously important."

So let's look at the scorecard: Who prevented war between India and Pakistan and is making both countries allies in the War on Terror? Who liberated Afghanistan and Iraq? Who forced Libya's cooperation to end its nuclear weapons program? Who has been the leader in encouraging Pakistan to unravel its own illegal nuclear arms proliferation? In every case, the answer is not the UN and not the EU. The answer is the United States and its various independent coalitions of willing allies. That is the way forward.

As I hope this book has made clear, the United Nations and the European Union, despite their pretensions to superiority are, in fact, morally bankrupt. It is the United States that truly is the leader of the free world and that, unlike the UN and the EU, is unwilling to kowtow to tyranny and terrorism. Not only should an American president not defer to the United Nations, to do so would violate his primary duty of protecting and defending the Constitution and the national security of our country.

In 1804, in a dispute between the United States and France, South Carolina patriot General Charles Pinckney declared the American credo: "Millions for defense, but not one cent for tribute." That should be the policy of every American president. We owe no tribute to the UN and the EU; we should look after our own defense.

The United Nations headquarters building in Manhattan is in the old neighborhood of Turtle Bay. Before John D. Rockefeller donated $8.5 million to buy it for the United Nations, Turtle Bay was an area of slaughterhouses and slums on the East River.[1] Now it is an international enclave, no longer American territory. It is elegant, but still politically and intellectually a slum. Turtle Bay needs to be reclaimed for America, and so does our foreign policy with Old Europe. President Bush has begun the process. Now is the time to finish the job.

ACKNOWLEDGMENTS

This book could never have been written without the patience and tireless support of my wife, Sharon, whose tolerance of my writing habits has been above and beyond the call of duty. I cannot fail to thank my good friend Ambassador Jose Sorzano for his insights on the UN and his humor and thoughtful guidance in helping define the UN's problems. My thanks to Harry Crocker—who helped shape the content of this book—and to Paula Decker and the rest of the crew at Regnery for their expertise in editing and producing this work.

THE FOLLOWING DOCUMENTS HAVE BEEN GATHERED FROM A NUMBER of sources—public and private, from both the U.S. government and foreign governments—in the course of the research on this book. You can see the UN's sprawling bureaucracy by glancing at the organizational chart. The first findings of the free Iraqi Governing Council's investigation, in letters to the UN, show the depth of the corruption in the UN Oil-for-Food scam. But the UN's most important failure—its tolerance, even support, of terrorism—is shown by much of what follows. From the picture of the Hezbollah and UN flags flying side-by-side, to a sworn affidavit that a UN agency hires terrorists, to a never-before-published CIA report connecting UN-affiliated NGOs directly to terrorists, the reader cannot avoid the conclusion that the UN cannot be trusted, far less relied on, in the war against terrorism and the states that support it.

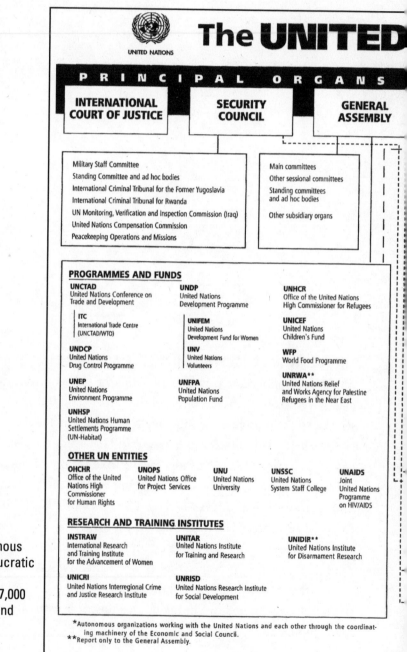

The enormous UN bureaucratic structure employs 17,000 people—and soaks up $1 billion each year.

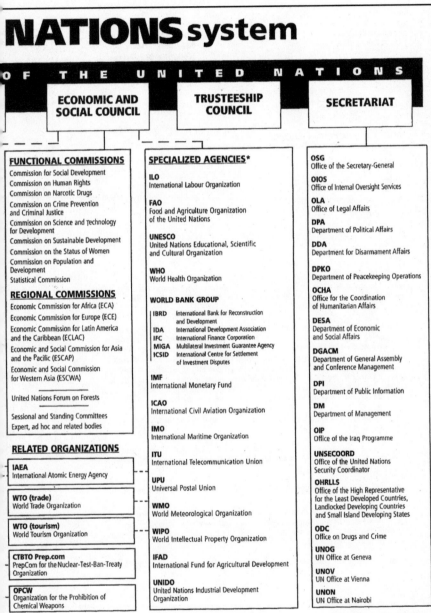

NATIONS system

OF THE UNITED NATIONS

ECONOMIC AND SOCIAL COUNCIL

TRUSTEESHIP COUNCIL

SECRETARIAT

FUNCTIONAL COMMISSIONS

Commission for Social Development
Commission on Human Rights
Commission on Narcotic Drugs
Commission on Crime Prevention and Criminal Justice
Commission on Science and Technology for Development
Commission on Sustainable Development
Commission on the Status of Women
Commission on Population and Development
Statistical Commission

REGIONAL COMMISSIONS

Economic Commission for Africa (ECA)
Economic Commission for Europe (ECE)
Economic Commission for Latin America and the Caribbean (ECLAC)
Economic and Social Commission for Asia and the Pacific (ESCAP)
Economic and Social Commission for Western Asia (ESCWA)

United Nations Forum on Forests

Sessional and Standing Committees
Expert, ad hoc and related bodies

RELATED ORGANIZATIONS

IAEA
International Atomic Energy Agency

WTO (trade)
World Trade Organization

WTO (tourism)
World Tourism Organization

CTBTO Prep.com
PrepCom for the Nuclear-Test-Ban-Treaty Organization

OPCW
Organization for the Prohibition of Chemical Weapons

SPECIALIZED AGENCIES*

ILO
International Labour Organization

FAO
Food and Agriculture Organization of the United Nations

UNESCO
United Nations Educational, Scientific and Cultural Organization

WHO
World Health Organization

WORLD BANK GROUP

IBRD	International Bank for Reconstruction and Development
IDA	International Development Association
IFC	International Finance Corporation
MIGA	Multilateral Investment Guarantee Agency
ICSID	International Centre for Settlement of Investment Disputes

IMF
International Monetary Fund

ICAO
International Civil Aviation Organization

IMO
International Maritime Organization

ITU
International Telecommunication Union

UPU
Universal Postal Union

WMO
World Meteorological Organization

WIPO
World Intellectual Property Organization

IFAD
International Fund for Agricultural Development

UNIDO
United Nations Industrial Development Organization

OSG
Office of the Secretary-General

OIOS
Office of Internal Oversight Services

OLA
Office of Legal Affairs

DPA
Department of Political Affairs

DDA
Department for Disarmament Affairs

DPKO
Department of Peacekeeping Operations

OCHA
Office for the Coordination of Humanitarian Affairs

DESA
Department of Economic and Social Affairs

DGACM
Department of General Assembly and Conference Management

DPI
Department of Public Information

DM
Department of Management

OIP
Office of the Iraq Programme

UNSECOORD
Office of the United Nations Security Coordinator

OHRLLS
Office of the High Representative for the Least Developed Countries, Landlocked Developing Countries and Small Island Developing States

ODC
Office on Drugs and Crime

UNOG
UN Office at Geneva

UNOV
UN Office at Vienna

UNON
UN Office at Nairobi

Published by the United Nations
Department of Public Information
DPI/2299 · February 2003

FROM:

Stanford Place   Telephone: 0044(1367) 240547
Faringdon   Telefax: 0044(1367) 242199
Oxon, SN7 8EX   E-mail: office@stanfordplace.com
England

TO: Secretary General to United Nations,
               Mr Kofi Annan

FAX: 001 212 963 1185

COPY TO: Foreign Secretary, Mr Jack Straw
               c/o Mr John Buck, Director, Iraq at the Foreign Office

FAX: 0207 008 4119

FROM: Claude Hankes-Drielsma   (Pages including this cover – 2)

DATE: 5 December 2003

IRAQ

I am in Baghdad this week to help and advise Ministers of the Governing Council. I made a courtesy call to Sir Jeremy Greenstock, offered to see Mr Bremer but his schedule did not allow. I had no formal meetings with the CPA but my path has crossed several of its members.

As a result of my findings here, combined with earlier information, I most strongly urge the UN to consider appointing an independent commission (to perhaps include a QC and a top accountant) to review and investigate the "Oil for Food Programme". The purpose being to identify and bring to account those that violated and profiteered by it or flaunted UN sanctions and in certain cases, I suspect, profiteer because and through sanctions. Were the UN to undertake this they would take the moral high ground and the initiative in demonstrating to the world that those guilty will be brought to account. It would be a most powerful message for the future.

Failure to do so might bring into question the UN's credibility and the public's perception of it.

The UN might also consider what action it can take with those countries not acting in good faith at the present time and with funds still held resulting from the "Oil for Food Programme."

My belief is that serious transgressions have taken place and may still be taking place.

A further issue which needs serious consideration and on which I would welcome an early discussion with you is how any debt which might have been incurred by Iraq post UN sanctions or made to rogue nations should be treated. This would be a further opportunity to send a powerful message for the future.

I look forward to your response and to meeting you again soon.

Letter from Roland Berger UK chairman Claude Hankes-Drielsma to Kofi Annan, requesting that the secretary-general allow an independent review of the Oil-for-Food program. Annan never responded.

TO: Mr Hans Corell, Under Secretary For Legal Affairs and Legal Counsel of the United Nations for: The Secretary General

Copy to : The Iraq Governing Council;   The Foreign Secretary, Mr Jack Straw,   co Mr John Buck, Director, Iraq at the Foreign Office.

FROM: Claude Hankes-Drielsma, Advisor to Iraq and Chairman of Roland Berger UK

Stanford Place
Faringdon
Oxon SN7 8EX

England.   **Urgent**

Tel: 01367 240547
Fax: 01367 242853
E-mail: office@stanfordplace.com

UNITED NATIONS INDEPENDENT INQUIRY

Dear Mr Corell,

Further to our conversation at the request of The Secretary General in response to my fax to him dated 5th December, I am now in a position to respond. There is information which I was not in position to refer to when we spoke.

The areas which need urgent investigation should include:

1. Oil for Food Program

   a. Indications are that not less than 10% was added to the value of all invoices to provide cash to Saddam Hussein (as much as $4 billion). If so, why was this not identified and prevented? Was the UN alerted to this at any stage? What action was taken and who was made aware of this allegation ?

A second letter from Hankes-Drielsma to UN official Hans Corell urges the need for an independent investigation into the Oil-for-Food program.

b. The UN received a fee of 2% of the value of all transactions to administer the program (as much as 1.1 Billion US Dollars). What method was put in place by the UN to insure inspection of the quality of food?

c. What controls where in place to monitor BNP (the bank in France) who handled the bulk of LC's, the total value of which may have in the region of 47 billion US$. What exchange rates were applied by BNP and why were payments converted into Euros and then back into US$?

d. The Role of Jordanian Banks such as Jordan National Bank, Arab Bank and Housing Bank: Have there been a proper independent audit of all transactions and a proper accounting of all funds? Are these banks still holding funds, if so how much, why and how is this monitored ? Was there a link between these banks and The Iraq Secret Service or any other part of the Saddam Hussein system?

e. Who at the UN carried overall responsibility for the Oil for Food program? Could there have been any link, directly or indirectly, with Saddam Hussein or his middle men?

2. UN approval of Oil Contracts under the above program

a. Why did the UN approve oil contracts to non-end users? And without knowing at what price?

b. A list of some of these contracts has been published by an Arab News Paper (this list which is known to me). It demonstrates beyond any doubt that Saddam Hussein bought political and other support under the aegis of the UN. In this list a "Mr. Sevan" is shown as receiving crude oil by this method through Panama.

c. VERY SIGNIFICANT SUPPLIES OF CRUDE OIL MADE TO NON-END USERS WERE TO OR TO THOSE LINKED TO INDIVIDUALS WITH POLITICAL INFLUENCE IN MANY COUNTRIES INCLUDING FRANCE AND JORDAN. WHAT METHOD OF CONTROL AND TRANSPARENCY OVER SALES DID THE UN REQUIRE?

I again urge the UN Secretary General to immediately appoint an independent commission.

21/04/2004

Press Release
SC/8064

SECURITY COUNCIL ADOPTS RESOLUTION WELCOMING APPOINTMENT

OF INQUIRY INTO IRAQ 'OIL-FOR-FOOD' PROGRAMME

Concerned by allegations regarding the administration and management of the United Nations "oil-for-food" programme, the Security Council this afternoon welcomed the Secretary-General's appointment of an independent high-level inquiry to investigate the matter.

Unanimously adopting resolution 1538 (2004), the Council also called on the Coalition Provisional Authority, Iraq and all other Member States, including their national regulatory authorities, to cooperate fully by all appropriate means with the inquiry.

The members of the inquiry are Paul Volcker, former Chairman of the United States Federal Reserve; Mark Pieth of Switzerland, an expert on money-laundering in the Organization for Economic Cooperation and Development (OECD); and Richard Goldstone of South Africa, former Prosecutor of the International Criminal Tribunals for the former Yugoslavia and Rwanda.

Begun in 1996, the United Nations oil-for-food programme allowed Iraq to use a portion of its petroleum revenues to purchase humanitarian relief. The effort was monitored by the Security Council's "661" committee, which included representatives from all 15 Council members.

Until its termination in November 2003, the programme oversaw the delivery of some $39 billion in humanitarian assistance to about 22 million people, many of whom were largely dependent on outside aid to survive since normal economic activity was severely constrained by sanctions imposed after Iraq's 1990 invasion of Kuwait.

The meeting began at 12:08 p.m. and ended at 12:10 p.m.

Council Resolution

Following is the full text of Security Council resolution 1538 (2004):

"*The Security Council*,

"*Expressing* the desire to see a full and fair investigation of efforts by the former Government of Iraq, including through bribery, kickbacks, surcharges on oil sales, and illicit payments in regard to purchases of humanitarian goods, to evade the provisions of resolution 661 (1990) of 6 August 1990 and subsequent relevant resolutions;

"*Concerned* by public news reports and commentaries that have called into question the administration and management of the Oil-for-food Programme (hereinafter the Programme) established pursuant to resolution 986 (1995) of   14 April 1995 and subsequent relevant resolutions, including allegations of fraud and corruption;

"*Affirming* that any illicit activity by United Nations officials, personnel and agents, as well as contractors, including entities that have entered into contracts under the Programme, is unacceptable;

"*Emphasizing* the importance of full cooperation with the independent high-level inquiry by all United Nations officials and personnel, the Coalition Provisional Authority, Iraq, and all other MemberStates;

"*Affirming* the letter of its President of 31 March 2004 welcoming the Secretary-General's decision to create an independent high-level inquiry to investigate the administration and management of the Programme and *taking note* of the details relating to its organization and terms of reference;

"1.   *Welcomes* the appointment of the independent high-level inquiry;

"2.   *Calls upon* the Coalition Provisional Authority, Iraq, and all other MemberStates, including their national regulatory authorities, to cooperate fully by all appropriate means with the inquiry;

"3.   *Looks forward* to receiving the inquiry's final report;

"4.   *Decides* to remain actively seized of the matter."

Kofi Annan finally agreed to an independent investigation of the Oil-for-Food program on April 21, 2004, four months after Hankes-Drielsma's first letter.

At Post Tziporen, on the Israeli-Lebanese border, the flag of the terrorist organization Hezbollah (right) flies fifteen feet from the UN flag.

2

Executive Summary

1. An archive consisting of documents, video cassettes and computer disks was captured by the IDF in the "Arab Liberation Front" (an organization under Iraqi patronage) and the Iraqi Ba'ath organization HQ in Ramallah. Other documents and videocassettes were captured during Operation Defensive Shield and in the ALF office in Tulkarm. The captured materials shed light on the **Iraqi aid to the Palestinian confrontation, with emphasis on the encouragement of terrorist attacks.** This aid, which is transferred in coordination with the PA and the Palestinian terrorist organizations, is an expression of Iraqi policy – the interest to **escalate the Israeli-Palestinian conflict,** inter alia, in order to **strengthen** Iraq's status among the Palestinians and in the Arab world, to **divert** international attention from Iraq and to **delay** US attack plans against Iraq. According to the captured documents, **this Iraqi interest gained momentum after Operation Defensive Shield.**

5. In the framework of the systematic Iraqi financial aid to the families of Palestinians killed in the violent confrontation (including the families of Israeli Arabs killed in the October 2000 events), the families of suicide terrorists receive **enlarged grants** from Saddam Hussein (**$25,000** for such a family, in contrast with **$10,000** for the family of an "ordinary" killed Palestinian terrorist). The captured documents demonstrate that the **intentional "gap"** in favor of the suicide terrorists' families **continued growing** as the Intifada went on. The fact that such large sums of money, in Palestinian terms, are distributed to the families of suicide terrorists (about nine years of work, from all the aid bodies) **encourages the suicide phenomenon.** It is an important (but not the only) consideration in the suicide terrorist's decision.

Pages from an Israeli Defense Force report, outlining Iraqi aid to Palestinian terrorists.

7.   While the "Arab Liberation Front" and the Ba'ath party in the PA areas are used by Iraq as "payment contractors" in the framework of the terrorism encouragement policy, the Iraqi regime uses another terrorist organization, the **"Palestinian Liberation Front"** headed by Muhammad Zaydan (**Abu al-Abbas**), as an **operational tool** for carrying out **terrorist attacks** against Israel. This organization, which carried out the terrorist attack aboard the *Achille Lauro* ship in 1986, in which a US citizen was murdered, is operated by the Iraqis in the PA areas.

9.   **The Palestinian Authority, on its part, enables the Iraqi regime (as well as other foreign entities) to freely implement the policy of encouraging the suicide attacks.** The PA security apparatuses and the **Fatah organization** are integrated into the network of money payments to the families of the killed terrorists, including the families of the suicide terrorists. The PA and the Fatah also enable the Iraqi regime to freely operate in the realm of **political propaganda** (this activity includes, inter alia, the dissemination of Iraqi messages calling to **continue the Intifada**, promoting the personality cult of **Saddam Hussein**, who enjoys popularity in Palestinian society, and dissemination of virulent and false **anti-American propaganda**).

10.   The Iraqi aid uncovered in the captured material is an additional significant and central component in the **external military, financial and logistic aid circles** constantly nourishing Palestinian terror. Such large-scope financial aid, as demonstrated in the documents captured in Operation Defensive Shield, is also provided by **Iran, Syria and Saudi Arabia.** Each of these countries adds fuel to the fire of the violence and terror in the PA in its own way and using its own methods. The **financial aid** is a central tool for encouraging terror in general, and **suicide terror** in particular. This **external aid has a strategic significance**, and, if not stopped, or at least significantly reduced, it will be difficult to end the violence and the terror produced by the PA and Palestinian society.

IDF/MI

"We are glad of the Istishhadiyyah [suicide] and heroic spirit of the Palestinian people. By Allah, what the Palestinian people does is beyond my expectations..." [Iraqi TV, 4 March 2002]

بنك الاستثمار الفلسطيني
Palestine Investment Bank
899 - Albireh   20000399
فرع البيرة

A/C : 02-02-040-04198515
ID#:   0
TEL : 0000000000

PAY TO, OR ORDER   ادفعوا لأمر   خالديه اسماعيل عبد العزيز الحوراني

THE SUM OF   سبعة حمسة وعشرين ألف دولار $ 25000 =

SIGNATURE   التوقيع   DATE   التاريخ

⑈20000399 ⑈76⑈89902⑈ 0400419851⑈

"The President Saddam Hussein's Grant" to the families of suicide terrorists in the framework of the Iraqi "terror industry" in the PA areas: a **$25,000 check**, which was transferred on 23 June 2002 to **Khaldiya Isma'il Abd Al-Aziz Al-Hurani**, mother of **the Hamas terrorist Fuad Isma'il Ahmad Al-Hurani**, who carried out a suicide attack on 9 March 2002 in the *Moment* cafe in Jerusalem. **11 Israelis were killed and 16 wounded** in the attack.

Courtesy of Israeli Defense forces

This check, drawn on the Palestine Investment Bank, was paid to the family of a suicide bomber. Saddam Hussein supported such terrorism by giving money to the bombers' families.

10.   Humanitarian and charitable institutions throughout Palestine employ personnel regardless of secturian or political affiliation and offer services on a similar basis. Thus, UNRWA. NGO-run and public hospitals and clinics, for example, employ members of different political groups such as Fatah. the PFLP, Hamas and Islamic Jihad, without reference to their belonging to a specific group. It would be impossible to do otherwise in the case of a group like Hamas, since it has the support of from 15-20% of the Palestinian population in the most reliable independent polling over the past 6-7 years, when regular polling began.

Affidavit of Rashid Khalidi, a leading Middle East scholar. He attests that UN-supported organizations such as UNRWA actively hire terrorists.

A student's notebook found in a UNRWA school. On it is written "Palestine," "Fatah the Revolution," and "Jerusalem is ours." The gunman on the back cover of the notebook partially obscures the UNRWA logo

An example of the way hostile, anti-West messages are spread in UNRWA-run schools is the ceremonial presentation of a shield to a senior Palestinian official. The shield pictured here bears a map of Palestine in the colors of the Palestinian flag. The message, popularized throughout Palestinian areas, is very clear: The whole area of Palestine belongs to the Palestinians and there is no place for the existence of a State of Israel. This message is given the apparent support of UNRWA by the use of its emblem, seen in the lower right corner.

This shield was presented to the Palestinian Authority's undersecretary of culture, Yahya Yakhluf. Its inscription reads: "In the name of the merciful and compassionate God Undersecretary (in charge) of the Ministry of Culture Yahya Yakhluf, as a sign of appreciation for your extraordinary support."

Yahya Yakhluf is a member of the terrorist organization Fatah.

OF THE 250 LOCAL AND FOREIGN-BASED NONGOVERNMENTAL
CHARITABLE ORGANIZATIONS (NGOS) THAT OPERATE WORLDWIDE, OVER 50
ARE INTERNATIONAL ISLAMIC NGOS CONDUCTING HUMANITARIAN WORK.
AVAILABLE INFORMATION INDICATES THAT APPROXIMATELY ONE THIRD OF
THESE ISLAMIC NGOS SUPPORT TERRORIST GROUPS OR EMPLOY INDIVIDUALS
WHO ARE SUSPECTED OF HAVING TERRORIST CONNECTIONS.
THIS REPORT DESCRIBES THE TERRORIST-RELATED ACTIVITIES AND
LINKAGES AMONG 15 OF THESE NGOS OPERATING IN OTHER PART OF THE
WORLD. INDIVIDUALS CONNECTED TO SOME OF THESE NGOS HAVE PLOTTED
TO KIDNAP OR KILL U.S. PERSONNEL.

GOVERNMENTS IN THE ISLAMIC WORLD GENERALLY SUPPORT THE MAJOR
CHARITIES' RELIGIOUS ACTIVITIES AND HELP FINANCE THEM, BUT ARE
UNABLE TO MONITOR THE GROUPS OR CONTROL HOW THEY USE THEIR MONEY.
THESE GOVERNMENTS RELY ON THE NGOS TO COLLECT AND DISTRIBUTE MUCH
OF THE HUMANITARIAN AID GIVEN TO REFUGEES AND DISPLACED PERSONS.
LEADERS OF COUNTRIES WHERE ISLAMIC NGOS ARE BASED OR OPERATE ARE
UNLIKELY TO TAKE MAJOR STEPS TO STOP THE ORGANIZATIONS'
ACTIVITIES UNLESS THEY BELIEVE THAT THESE GROUPS THREATEN THEIR
OWN STABILITY OR ARE DAMAGING IMPORTANT BILATERAL OR MULTILATERAL
RELATIONSHIPS.

A GROWING BODY OF REPORTING INDICATES THAT SOME OF THESE
CHARITIES ARE BEING USED TO AID ISLAMIC EXTREMIST GROUPS THAT
ENGAGE IN TERRORISM. WE HAVE INFORMATION THAT NEARLY ONE THIRD
OF THE ISLAMIC NGOS IN THE BALKANS HAVE FACILITATED THE
ACTIVITIES OF ISLAMIC GROUPS THAT ENGAGE IN TERRORISM, INCLUDING
THE EGYPTIAN AL-GAMA'AT AL-ISLAMIYYA, PALESTINIAN HAMAS, ALGERIAN
GROUPS, AND LEBANESE HIZBALLAH. SOME OF THE TERRORIST GROUPS,
SUCH AS AL-GAMA'AT, HAVE ACCESS TO CREDENTIALS FOR THE UN HIGH
COMMISSION FOR REFUGEES AND OTHER UN STAFFS IN THE FORMER
YUGOSLAVIA.

ARREST INDIVIDUAL MEMBERS. SOME COUNTRIES HAVE CONTINUED TO
ALLOW SUSPECT NGOS TO OPERATE WHILE ARRESTING INDIVIDUAL MEMBERS
FOR TERRORISM OR OTHER ILLEGAL ACTS. THIS TACTIC, WHEN APPLIED
CONSISTENTLY, APPEARS TO BE THE MOST SUCCESSFUL IN HALTING
ILLEGAL ACTIVITIES WITHIN NGOS. FOR EXAMPLE, POLICE IN THE
PHILIPPINES HAVE BEEN INVESTIGATING PEOPLE AND ORGANIZATIONS,
INCLUDING NGOS, INVOLVED IN PLOTS AGAINST WESTERN AIRLINERS,
AMBASSADORS, THE POPE, AND PHILIPPINE OFFICIALS SINCE JANUARY
1995. THESE INVESTIGATIONS HAVE LED TO PERIODIC ARRESTS AND
APPEAR TO HAVE PREVENTED SOME NGOS, INCLUDING THE INTERNATIONAL
ISLAMIC RELIEF ORGANIZATION, FROM CONTINUING TO BE USED AS COVER
FOR ILLICIT ACTIVITIES. THE PHILIPPINE GOVERNMENT HAS ESCAPED
CONDEMNATION FOR ITS EFFORTS BY ALL BUT EXTREMIST ISLAMIC GROUPS
AND APPEARS TO HAVE FOILED, TO DATE, ANY ATTEMPTS BY THOSE GROUPS
TO EXACT REVENGE.

Excerpts from a never-before-published CIA document. The report details
the connection many Non-Governmental Organizations (NGOs) have with terrorist groups. Some of these NGOs are even supported by Arab governments
such as Saudi Arabia, and some have direct links to the UN itself.

-- INTERNATIONAL ISLAMIC RELIEF ORGANIZATION (IIRO)

-- ARABIC NAME: HAY'AT AL-IGHATHA AL-ISLAMIYYA AL-'ALAMIYYA.

-- AKA: IGHATHA OR IGASA.

-- OFFICES: ZAGREB, SARAJEVO, SPLIT, LJUBLJANA, AND TUZLA; ALSO
IN VIENNA, AUSTRIA. OPERATES IN CELIC, GRACANICA, ZIVINICE,
SREBRENIK, BANOVICI, KALESIJA, AND TEOCAK. HEADQUARTERS IN
JIDDAH, SAUDI ARABIA. THE IIRO IS AFFILIATED WITH THE MUSLIM
WORLD LEAGUE (MWL), A MAJOR INTERNATIONAL ORGANIZATION LARGELY
FINANCED BY THE GOVERNMENT OF SAUDI ARABIA. LAST YEAR, THE HEAD
OF THE MWL, WHO IS APPOINTED BY KING FAHD, WAS ALSO CHAIRMAN OF
THE BOARD OF TRUSTEES OF THE IIRO, ACCORDING TO IIRO LITERATURE.
THE IIRO HAS OFFICES IN OVER 90 COUNTRIES.

-- EXTREMIST CONNECTIONS: HAMAS, ALGERIANS, AL-GAMA'AT
AL-ISLAMIYYA. RAMZI AHMED YOUSEF, WHO IS AWAITING TRIAL IN NEW
YORK FOR HIS SUSPECTED INVOLVEMENT IN THE WORLD TRADE CENTER
BOMBING. USAMA BIN LADIN, A WEALTHY SAUDI-BORN BUSINESSMAN
CURRENTLY RESIDING IN SUDAN WHO SUPPORTS VARIOUS ISLAMIC
EXTREMIST GROUPS.

-- SUPPORT FOR EXTREMIST/TERRORIST ACTIVITY: THE REGIONAL
FINANCIAL ACCOUNTANT FOR THE IIRO, AN EGYPTIAN NAMED HOSSAM
MEAWAD MOHAMMAD ALI, WAS DETAINED BY CROATIAN AUTHORITIES IN A
RAID IN ZAGREB IN APRIL 1995 AND HAS RELOCATED TO LJUBLJANA,
ACCORDING TO A FOREIGN GOVERNMENT SERVICE. THE MACEDONIAN
GOVERNMENT CLOSED THE IIRO OFFICE IN SKOPJE IN MARCH 1995 FOR
AIDING ALBANIAN ETHNIC POLITICAL PARTIES AND THE ALBANIAN ISLAMIC
YOUTH ORGANIZATION. THE FORMER HEAD OF THE IIRO OFFICE IN THE
PHILIPPINES, MOHAMMAD JAMAL KHALIFA, HAS BEEN LINKED TO MANILA-
BASED PLOTS TO TARGET THE POPE AND US AIRLINES; HIS BROTHER-IN-
LAW IS USAMA BIN LADIN. ANOTHER HIGH-RANKING OFFICIAL IN THE
PHILIPPINES LEADS HAMAS MEETINGS, AND THE MAJORITY OF HAMAS
MEMBERS IN THE PHILIPPINES ARE EMPLOYED BY THE ORGANIZATION. THE
IIRO HELPS FUND SIX MILITANT TRAINING CAMPS IN AFGHANISTAN,
ACCORDING TO A CLANDESTINE SOURCE.

-- LINKS TO OTHER NGOS: COORDINATION COUNCIL, HRA, THIRD WORLD
RELIEF AGENCY, QATAR CHARITABLE SOCIETY, KJRC, SAUDI HIGH
COMMISSION.

The NGO International Islamic Relief Organization is linked to
Ramzi Yousef, on trial for his role in the 1993 World Trade Center
bombing, and Osama bin Laden.

MAKHTAB AL-KHIDAMAT (MAK)

-- AKA: HUMAN SERVICES ORGANIZATION/OFFICE (HSO), AL-KIFAH.

-- OFFICES: ZAGREB AND SARAJEVO. HEADQUARTERS IN PESHAWAR,
PAKISTAN.

-- EXTREMIST CONNECTIONS: ALGERIAN GROUPS, AFGHAN VETERANS,
RAMZI YOUSEF, USAMA BIN LADIN, AND POSSIBLY HIZBALLAH, AND
AL-GAMA'AT AL-ISLAMIYYA.

-- SUPPORT TO EXTREMIST/TERRORIST ACTIVITY: ACCORDING TO A
FOREIGN GOVERNMENT SERVICE, THE FORMER DIRECTOR OF THE ZAGREB
OFFICE OF HSO AND HIS DEPUTY WERE BOTH SENIOR MEMBERS OF ALGERIAN
EXTREMIST GROUPS; FRENCH POLICE ARRESTED THE DEPUTY FOR WEAPONS
SMUGGLING IN FRANCE IN JULY 1994, ACCORDING TO A FRENCH LAW
ENFORCEMENT OFFICIAL. ANOTHER FOREIGN GOVERNMENT SERVICE
REPORTED THAT AN ALGERIAN NATIONAL AFFILIATED WITH HSO AND A
SENIOR COMMANDER OF THE MUJAHEDIN, ALSO ALGERIAN, WERE PREPARING
FOR AN UNSPECIFIED TERRORIST ATTACK IN EUROPE IF SHAYKH UMAR ABD
AL-RAHMAN, THEN ON TRIAL IN NEW YORK FOR COMPLICITY IN THE 1993
WORLD TRADE CENTER BOMBING, WERE CONVICTED. THE SHAYKH WAS
CONVICTED IN OCTOBER 1995 OF CONSPIRACY TO COMMIT TERRORIST ACTS
IN THE UNITED STATES. HE WAS SENTENCED TO LIFE IN PRISON WITHOUT
PAROLE ON 17 JANUARY 1996. IN APRIL 1995 THE CROATIAN SERVICE
DETAINED AN ALGERIAN EMPLOYEE OF THE HSO WHO HAD IN HIS
POSSESSION PASSPORTS OF ARAB INDIVIDUALS IN BOSNIA, INCLUDING AN
EMPLOYEE OF THE THIRD WORLD RELIEF AGENCY, ACCORDING TO THE
SECOND SERVICE. THE PRESS HAS REPORTED THAT SOME EMPLOYEES OF
MAK'S NEW YORK BRANCH WERE INVOLVED IN THE WORLD TRADE CENTER
BOMBING. THE PESHAWAR OFFICE FUNDS AT LEAST NINE TRAINING CAMPS
IN AFGHANISTAN, ACCORDING TO CLANDESTINE SOURCES.

-- LINKS TO OTHER NGOS: TWRA, IIRO. MAK IS SUSPECTED OF HAVING
LINKS TO THE MUSLIM WORLD LEAGUE.

Another "charity" suspected of ties to terrorist acts, including the 1993
World Trade Center bombing.

HUMAN APPEAL INTERNATIONAL (HAI)

-- ARABIC NAME: HAY'AT AL-A'MAL AL-KHAYRIYYA.

-- AKA: CHARITABLE WORKS ORGANIZATION/COMMITTEE, CHARITY ORGANIZATION (ORIGINAL NAME).

-- OFFICES: ZAGREB AND TUZLA. HEADQUARTERED IN DUBAI, UNITED ARAB EMIRATES. OTHER OFFICES IN SIDON, KHARTOUM, NOUAKCHOTT, MAURITANIA, AND ALSO IN DENMARK, TURKEY, AND THE UNITED KINGDOM.

-- EXTREMIST CONNECTIONS: HAMAS.

-- SUPPORT TO EXTREMIST/TERRORIST ACTIVITIES: AMONG OTHER ACTIVITIES, THIS ORGANIZATION PROBABLY ACTS AS A FUND-RAISER FOR HAMAS, ACCORDING TO A FOREIGN GOVERNMENT SERVICE.

-- LINKS TO OTHER NGOS: COORDINATION COUNCIL, HUMAN RELIEF INTERNATIONAL (HRI), MUWAFAQ, QATAR CHARITABLE SOCIETY.

Human Appeal International is a "donor and partner" of the UN High Commission for Refugees (UNHCR). It also raises money for Hamas.

```
ISLAMIC RELIEF AGENCY (ISRA)

--  AKA:  IARA, YARA, AFRICAN ISLAMIC RELIEF AGENCY.

--  OFFICES:  SARAJEVO, ZAGREB, TIRANA, TUZLA, KALESIJA, AND
UNSPECIFIED CITIES IN GERMANY.  OPERATES IN KALESIJA, BANOVICI,
DOBOJ EAST, AND ZVORNIK.  BASED IN KHARTOUM, SUDAN.  OFFICES IN
30 COUNTRIES WORLDWIDE.

--  EXTREMIST CONNECTIONS:  SUDAN.

--  SUPPORT TO EXTREMIST/TERRORIST ACTIVITY:  THE ISRA OFFICE IN
ZAGREB PROVIDES WEAPONS TO THE BOSNIAN MILITARY, ACCORDING TO A
CLANDESTINE SOURCE.  THE SOURCE CLAIMED THE OFFICE WAS CONTROLLED
BY OFFICIALS OF SUDAN'S RULING PARTY, THE NATIONAL ISLAMIC FRONT.

--  LINKS TO OTHER NGOS:  THIRD WORLD RELIEF AGENCY.
```

The Islamic Relief Agency is another "donor and partner" of the UNHCR, and is reportedly controlled by the Sudanese government.

NATIONAL STRATEGY TO
COMBAT WEAPONS
OF MASS
DESTRUCTION

DECEMBER 2002

Before America's break with the UN over Operation Iraqi Freedom, the Bush administration issued this strategy for combating WMD.

National Strategy to Combat Weapons of Mass Destruction

"The gravest danger our Nation faces lies at the crossroads of radicalism and technology. Our enemies have openly declared that they are seeking weapons of mass destruction, and evidence indicates that they are doing so with determination. The United States will not allow these efforts to succeed. ...History will judge harshly those who saw this coming danger but failed to act. In the new world we have entered, the only path to peace and security is the path of action."

PRESIDENT BUSH
THE NATIONAL SECURITY STRATEGY OF THE UNITED STATES OF AMERICA
SEPTEMBER 17, 2002

INTRODUCTION

Weapons of mass destruction (WMD)—nuclear, biological, and chemical—in the possession of hostile states and terrorists represent one of the greatest security challenges facing the United States. We must pursue a comprehensive strategy to counter this threat in all of its dimensions.

An effective strategy for countering WMD, including their use and further proliferation, is an integral component of the National Security Strategy of the United States of America. As with the war on terrorism, our strategy for homeland security, and our new concept of deterrence, the U.S. approach to combat WMD represents a fundamental change from the past. To succeed, we must take full advantage of today's opportunities, including the application of new technologies, increased emphasis on intelligence collection and analysis, the strengthening of alliance relationships, and the establishment of new partnerships with former adversaries.

Weapons of mass destruction could enable adversaries to inflict massive harm on the United States, our military forces at home and abroad, and our friends and allies. Some states, including several that have supported and continue to support terrorism, already possess WMD and are seeking even greater capabilities, as tools of coercion and intimidation. For them, these are not weapons of last resort, but militarily useful weapons of choice intended to overcome our nation's advantages in conventional forces and to deter us from responding to aggression against our friends and allies in regions of vital interest. In addition, terrorist groups are seeking to acquire WMD with the stated purpose of killing large numbers of our people and those of friends and allies—without compunction and without warning.

We will not permit the world's most dangerous regimes and terrorists to threaten us with the world's most destructive weapons. We must accord the highest priority to the protection of the United States, our forces, and our friends and allies from the existing and growing WMD threat.

PILLARS OF OUR NATIONAL STRATEGY

Our National Strategy to Combat Weapons of Mass Destruction has three principal pillars:

Counterproliferation to Combat WMD Use

The possession and increased likelihood of use of WMD by hostile states and terrorists are realities of the contemporary security environment. It is therefore critical that the U.S. military and appropriate civilian agencies be prepared to deter and defend against the full range of possible WMD employment scenarios. We will ensure that all needed capabilities to combat WMD are fully integrated into the emerging defense transformation plan and into our homeland security posture. Counterproliferation will also be fully integrated into the basic doctrine, training, and equipping of all forces, in order to ensure that they can sustain operations to decisively defeat WMD-armed adversaries.

Strengthened Nonproliferation to Combat WMD Proliferation

The United States, our friends and allies, and the broader international community must undertake every effort to prevent states and terrorists from acquiring WMD and missiles. We must enhance traditional measures—diplomacy, arms control, multilateral agreements, threat reduction assistance, and export controls—that seek to dissuade or impede proliferant states and terrorist networks, as well as to slow and make more costly their access to sensitive technologies, material, and expertise. We must ensure compliance with relevant international agreements, including the Nuclear Nonproliferation Treaty (NPT), the Chemical Weapons Convention (CWC), and the Biological Weapons Convention (BWC). The United States will continue to work with other states to improve their capability to prevent unauthorized transfers of WMD and missile technology, expertise, and material. We will identify and pursue new methods of prevention, such as national criminalization of proliferation activities and expanded safety and security measures.

Consequence Management to Respond to WMD Use

Finally, the United States must be prepared to respond to the use of WMD against our citizens, our military forces, and those of friends and allies. We will develop and maintain the capability to reduce to the extent possible the potentially horrific consequences of WMD attacks at home and abroad.

The three pillars of the U.S. national strategy to combat WMD are seamless elements of a comprehensive approach. Serving to integrate the pillars are four cross-cutting enabling functions that need to be pursued on a priority basis: intelligence collection and analysis on WMD, delivery systems, and related technologies; research and development to improve our ability to respond to evolving threats; bilateral and multilateral cooperation; and targeted strategies against hostile states and terrorists.

COUNTERPROLIFERATION

We know from experience that we cannot always be successful in preventing and containing the proliferation of WMD to hostile states and terrorists. Therefore, U.S. military and appropriate civilian agencies must possess the full range of operational capabilities to counter the threat and use of WMD by states and terrorists against the United States, our military forces, and friends and allies.

Interdiction

Effective interdiction is a critical part of the U.S. strategy to combat WMD and their delivery means. We must enhance the capabilities of our military, intelligence, technical, and law enforcement communities to prevent the movement of WMD materials, technology, and expertise to hostile states and terrorist organizations.

Deterrence

Today's threats are far more diverse and less predictable than those of the past. States hostile to the United States and to our friends and allies have demonstrated their willingness to take high risks to achieve their goals, and are aggressively pursuing WMD and their means of delivery as critical tools in this effort. As a consequence, we require new methods of deterrence. A strong declaratory policy and effective military forces are essential elements of our contemporary deterrent posture, along with the full range of political tools to persuade potential adversaries not to seek or use WMD. The United States will continue to make clear that it reserves the right to respond with overwhelming force—including through resort to all of our options—to the use of WMD against the United States, our forces abroad, and friends and allies.

In addition to our conventional and nuclear response and defense capabilities, our overall deterrent posture against WMD threats is reinforced by effective intelligence, surveillance, interdiction, and domestic law enforcement capabilities. Such combined capabilities enhance deterrence both by devaluing an adversary's WMD and missiles, and by posing the prospect of an overwhelming response to any use of such weapons.

Defense and Mitigation

Because deterrence may not succeed, and because of the potentially devastating consequences of WMD use against our forces and civilian population, U.S. military forces and appropriate civilian agencies must have the capability to defend against WMD-armed adversaries, including in appropriate cases through preemptive measures. This requires capabilities to detect and destroy an adversary's WMD assets before these weapons are used. In addition, robust active and passive defenses and mitigation measures must be in place to enable U.S. military forces and appropriate civilian agencies to accomplish their missions, and to assist friends and allies when WMD are used.

Active defenses disrupt, disable, or destroy WMD en route to their targets. Active defenses include vigorous air defense and effective missile defenses against today's threats. Passive defenses must be tailored to the unique characteristics of the various forms of WMD. The United States must also have the ability rapidly and effectively to mitigate the effects of a WMD attack against our deployed forces.

Our approach to defend against biological threats has long been based on our approach to chemical threats, despite the fundamental differences between these weapons. The United States is developing a new approach to provide us and our friends and allies with an effective defense against biological weapons.

Finally, U.S. military forces and domestic law enforcement agencies as appropriate must stand ready to respond against the source of any WMD attack. The primary objective of a response is to disrupt an imminent attack or an attack in progress, and eliminate the threat of future attacks. As with deterrence and prevention, an effective response requires rapid attribution and robust strike capability. We must accelerate efforts to field new capabilities to defeat WMD-related assets. The United States needs to be prepared to conduct post-conflict operations to destroy or dismantle any residual WMD capabilities of the hostile state or terrorist network. An effective U.S. response not only will eliminate the source of a WMD attack but will also have a powerful deterrent effect upon other adversaries that possess or seek WMD or missiles.

NONPROLIFERATION

Active Nonproliferation Diplomacy

The United States will actively employ diplomatic approaches in bilateral and multilateral settings in pursuit of our nonproliferation goals.

We must dissuade supplier states from cooperating with proliferant states and induce proliferant states to end their WMD and missile programs. We will hold countries responsible for complying with their commitments. In addition, we will continue to build coalitions to support our efforts, as well as to seek their increased support for nonproliferation and threat reduction cooperation programs. However, should our wide-ranging nonproliferation efforts fail, we must have available the full range of operational capabilities necessary to defend against the possible employment of WMD.

Multilateral Regimes

Existing nonproliferation and arms control regimes play an important role in our overall strategy. The United States will support those regimes that are currently in force, and work to improve the effectiveness of, and compliance with, those regimes. Consistent with other policy priorities, we will also promote new agreements and arrangements that serve our nonproliferation goals. Overall, we seek to cultivate an international environment that is more conducive to nonproliferation. Our efforts will include:

- Nuclear
  - Strengthening of the Nuclear Nonproliferation Treaty and International Atomic Energy Agency (IAEA), including through ratification of an IAEA Additional Protocol by all NPT states parties, assurances that all states put in place full-scope IAEA safeguards agreements, and appropriate increases in funding for the Agency;
  - Negotiating a Fissile Material Cut-Off Treaty that advances U.S. security interests; and
  - Strengthening the Nuclear Suppliers Group and Zangger Committee.

- Chemical and Biological
  - Effective functioning of the Organization for the Prohibition of Chemical Weapons;
  - Identification and promotion of constructive and realistic measures to strengthen the BWC and thereby to help meet the biological weapons threat; and
  - Strengthening of the Australia Group.
- Missile
  - Strengthening the Missile Technology Control Regime (MTCR), including through support for universal adherence to the International Code of Conduct Against Ballistic Missile Proliferation.

Nonproliferation and Threat Reduction Cooperation

The United States pursues a wide range of programs, including the Nunn-Lugar program, designed to address the proliferation threat stemming from the large quantities of Soviet-legacy WMD and missile-related expertise and materials. Maintaining an extensive and efficient set of nonproliferation and threat reduction assistance programs to Russia and other former Soviet states is a high priority. We will also continue to encourage friends and allies to increase their contributions to these programs, particularly through the G-8 Global Partnership Against the Spread of Weapons and Materials of Mass Destruction. In addition, we will work with other states to improve the security of their WMD-related materials.

Controls on Nuclear Materials

In addition to programs with former Soviet states to reduce fissile material and improve the security of that which remains, the United States will continue to discourage the worldwide accumulation of separated plutonium and to minimize the use of highly-enriched uranium. As outlined in the National Energy Policy, the United States will work in collaboration with international partners to develop recycle and fuel treatment technologies that are cleaner, more efficient, less waste-intensive, and more proliferation-resistant.

U.S. Export Controls

We must ensure that the implementation of U.S. export controls furthers our nonproliferation and other national security goals, while recognizing the realities that American businesses face in the increasingly globalized marketplace.

We will work to update and strengthen export controls using existing authorities. We also seek new legislation to improve the ability of our export control system to give full weight to both nonproliferation objectives and commercial interests. Our overall goal is to focus our resources on truly sensitive exports to hostile states or those that engage in onward proliferation, while removing unnecessary barriers in the global marketplace.

Nonproliferation Sanctions

Sanctions can be a valuable component of our overall strategy against WMD proliferation. At times, however, sanctions have proven inflexible and ineffective. We will develop a comprehensive sanctions policy to better integrate sanctions into our overall strategy and work with Congress to consolidate and modify existing sanctions legislation.

WMD CONSEQUENCE MANAGEMENT

Defending the American homeland is the most basic responsibility of our government. As part of our defense, the United States must be fully prepared to respond to the consequences of WMD use on our soil, whether by hostile states or by terrorists. We must also be prepared to respond to the effects of WMD use against our forces deployed abroad, and to assist friends and allies.

The National Strategy for Homeland Security discusses U.S. Government programs to deal with the consequences of the use of a chemical, biolog-ical, radiological, or nuclear weapon in the United States. A number of these programs offer training, planning, and assistance to state and local governments. To maximize their effectiveness, these efforts need to be integrated and comprehensive. Our first responders must have the full range of protective, medical, and remediation tools to identify, assess, and respond rapidly to a WMD event on our territory.

The White House Office of Homeland Security will coordinate all federal efforts to prepare for and mitigate the consequences of terrorist attacks within the United States, including those involving WMD. The Office of Homeland Security will also work closely with state and local governments to ensure their planning, training, and equipment requirements are addressed. These issues, including the roles of the Department of Homeland Security, are addressed in detail in the National Strategy for Homeland Security.

The National Security Council's Office of Combating Terrorism coordinates and helps improve U.S. efforts to respond to and manage the recovery from terrorist attacks outside the United States. In cooperation with the Office of Combating Terrorism, the Department of State coordinates interagency efforts to work with our friends and allies to develop their own emergency preparedness and consequence management capabilities.

INTEGRATING THE PILLARS

Several critical enabling functions serve to integrate the three pillars—counterproliferation, nonproliferation, and consequence management —of the U.S. National Strategy to Combat WMD.

Improved Intelligence Collection and Analysis

A more accurate and complete understanding of the full range of WMD threats is, and will remain, among the highest U.S. intelligence priorities, to enable us to prevent proliferation, and to deter or defend against those who would use those capabilities against us. Improving our ability to obtain timely and accurate knowledge of adversaries' offensive and defensive capabilities, plans, and intentions is key to developing effective counter- and nonproliferation policies and capabilities. Particular emphasis must be accorded to improving: intelligence regarding WMD-related facilities and activities; interaction among U.S. intelligence, law enforcement, and military agencies; and intelligence cooperation with friends and allies.

Research and Development

The United States has a critical need for cutting-edge technology that can quickly and effectively detect, analyze, facilitate interdiction of, defend against, defeat, and mitigate the consequences of WMD. Numerous U.S. Government departments and agencies are currently engaged in the essential research and development to support our overall strategy against WMD proliferation.

The new Counterproliferation Technology Coordination Committee, consisting of senior representatives from all concerned agencies, will act to improve interagency coordination of U.S. Government counterproliferation research and development efforts. The Committee will assist in identifying priorities, gaps, and overlaps in existing programs and in examining options for future investment strategies.

Strengthened International Cooperation

WMD represent a threat not just to the United States, but also to our friends and allies and the broader international community. For this reason, it is vital that we work closely with like-minded countries on all elements of our comprehensive proliferation strategy.

Targeted Strategies Against Proliferants

All elements of the overall U.S. strategy to combat WMD must be brought to bear in targeted strategies against supplier and recipient states of WMD proliferation concern, as well as against terrorist groups which seek to acquire WMD.

A few states are dedicated proliferators, whose leaders are determined to develop, maintain, and improve their WMD and delivery capabilities, which directly threaten the United States, U.S. forces overseas, and/or our friends and allies. Because each of these regimes is different, we will pursue country-specific strategies that best enable us and our friends and allies to prevent, deter, and defend against WMD and missile threats from each of them. These strategies must also take into account the growing cooperation among proliferant states—so-called secondary proliferation—which challenges us to think in new ways about specific country strategies.

One of the most difficult challenges we face is to prevent, deter, and defend against the acquisition and use of WMD by terrorist groups. The current and potential future linkages between terrorist groups and state sponsors of terrorism are particularly dangerous and require priority attention. The full range of counterproliferation, nonproliferation, and consequence management measures must be brought to bear against the WMD terrorist threat, just as they are against states of greatest proliferation concern.

END NOTE

Our National Strategy to Combat WMD requires much of all of us—the Executive Branch, the Congress, state and local governments, the American people, and our friends and allies. The requirements to prevent, deter, defend against, and respond to today's WMD threats are complex and challenging. But they are not daunting. We can and will succeed in the tasks laid out in this strategy; we have no other choice.

CHAPTER TWO—THE UN: HANDMAIDEN OF TERRORISM

1. UN Charter, Article 25.
2. http://www.state.gov/t/us/rm/26129pf.htm.
3. Murray Weiss, "Subway Mystery: Iran Duo Caught Taping," *New York Post*, November 18, 2003.
4. Ibid.
5. Treasury Department press release, November 19, 2002.
6. Ibid.
7. http://www.strategicstudies.org/Balkans/Sep1703.htm.
8. Ibid.
9. The al-Qaeda cell that attacked the World Trade Center in 1993 trained there.
10. http://ods-dds ny.un.org/doc/UNDOC/GEN/N01/557/43/PDF/N0155734.pdf? OpenElement.
11. Geneva Convention for the Treatment of Prisoners of War, Article 4 (1949, adopted 1950). This definition is virtually identical to the one used by the U.S. Supreme Court in its decision *Ex Parte Quirin*, in which the military—not civilian—trial and execution of German terrorist agents landed covertly on U.S. soil was held constitutional. *Ex Parte Quirin*, 317 U.S. 1 (1942).
12. http://history1900s.about.com/gi/dynamic/offsite.htm?site=http%3A%2F%2Fwww.monde-diplomatique.fr%2Ffocus%2Fmideast%2Farafat74-en.
13. Israeli report, September 2002.
14. Ibid.
15. Ibid.
16. *Ha'Aretz Daily*, January 11, 2004.
17. www.un.org.
18. Anne Bayefsky, "How the U.N.'s Human Rights Investigations Do Yasser Arafat's Dirty Work," *New York Sun*, April 29, 2002.
19. www.un.org/UNRWA.
20. Khalidi affidavit. See also page 159.
21. Merkel speech, November 23, 2003.
22. Previously undisclosed CIA report.

CHAPTER THREE—"KOFIGATE": THE UN OIL-FOR-FOOD PROGRAM

1. Claudia Rosett, "Oil-for-Terror?" http://www.nationalreview.com/comment/rosett200404182336.asp.
2. Security Council Resolution 986.
3. Ibid.
4. Ibid.
5. UN press release, November 21, 2003.
6. Michael Soussan, "The Cash-for-Saddam Program," *Wall Street Journal*, March 8, 2004.
7. Ibid.
8. UN Statement, February 18, 2004; see also "Oil for Saddam," *Wall Street Journal*, February 20, 2004.
9. Ibid.
10. UN Security Council Resolution 1538, April 21, 2004.

CHAPTER FOUR—QUAGMIRE DIPLOMACY

1. Lt. General Thomas McInerney and Gen. Paul Vallely, *Endgame: The Bluprint for Victory in the War on Terror* (Washington, D.C.: Regnery, 2004), 80–82.
2. Sun Tzu, *The Art of War*, Griffith translation, (Oxford: Oxford University Press, 1963), 53.
3. According to CNN.

CHAPTER FIVE—SECRETARY-GENERAL KOFI ANNAN: A SYMPTOM OF THE UN DISEASE

1. Richard Butler, *The Greatest Threat: Iraq, Weapons of Mass Destruction, and the Growing Crisis of Global Security* (New York: Public Affairs Press, 2000), 1.
2. UN Security Council Resolution 687.
3. Jed Babbin, "No Prince Charming Here," *Washington Times*, October 29, 2002.
4. Butler, 136.
5. Ibid., 132.
6. UN Charter, Article 100.
7. Butler, 133.
8. Ibid., 138.
9. Ibid., 140.
10. Ibid., 141–143.
11. Ibid., 146.
12. Ibid., 185.
13. http://clinton4.nara.gov/WH/New/html/19981219-2655.html.
14. UN press release SG/SM/8581.
15. UN press release SG/T/2369.

16. http://www.un.org/law/icc/statute/romefra.htm.
17. Rome Statute, Article 8, section (b).
18. Kissinger, "The Pitfalls of Universal Jurisdiction," *Foreign Affairs*, July/August 2001.
19. Ibid.
20. BBC News, June 12, 2003.
21. Typical is the CBU-87/103, an unguided munition that dispenses 202 bomblets in a regular pattern. It was used extensively by U.S. Air Force and Navy aircraft in the 2003 Iraq campaign against troops and light armored vehicles.
22. Reuters, January 21, 2004.
23. Ibid.
24. Annan statement, December 16, 2003.
25. "Secretary-General Annan rejects any trial that could lead to Saddam's execution," Associated Press, December 15, 2003.
26. "Colin in Kofi Land," *Wall Street Journal*, October 13, 2003.
27. Ibid.
28. Annan statement at UN headquarters press conference, December 18, 2003.

CHAPTER SIX—THE UN BUREAUCRACY: NICE WORK IF YOU CAN GET IT

1. "UN System Funding: Congressional Issues," Congressional Research Service No. 1B86116, April 2, 2003.
2. Ibid.
3. Ibid.
4. "UN System Funding: Congressional Issues," 4.
5. *Wall Street Journal*, December 16, 2003.
6. Ibid.
7. See http://www.un.org/Depts/OHRM/salaries_allowances/salary.htm.
8. Ibid.
9. http://www.un.org/Overview/unmember.html.
10. *Wall Street Journal*, December 19, 2003.
11. Ibid.
12. CIA World Fact Book.
13. CRS report, April 2003.
14. Jose Sorzano, "The UN: Forty Years, Forty Facts," *National Interest*, Winter 1986.
15. Ibid.
16. "UN System Funding: Congressional Issues," 5.

CHAPTER SEVEN—THE UN'S FATAL FLAWS

1. Samuel Rosenman, ed., "Public Papers and Addresses of Franklin D. Roosevelt, vol. 10, 314, cited on http://usinfo.state.gov.
2. Ibid., 40.
3. Ibid., 41.

4. James Hume, *The Wit and Wisdom of Winston Churchill* (New York: Harper Collins, 1995), 180.

5. Samuel C. Schlesinger, *Act of Creation: The Founding of the United Nations* (Boulder, CO: Westview Press, 2003), 64.

6. Ibid., 7.

7. Ibid., 6.

8. The Security Council has been expanded, and now has fifteen members. The permanent five—America, Britain, Russia, China and France—are still the only ones who have the power to veto its resolutions.

9. UN Charter, Articles 5 and 6.

10. There is considerable debate as to whether Plato actually wrote this. It is not found in his *Dialogues*, but is found in the writings of George Santayana. MacArthur's attribution is most often cited, and may not be correct.

11. UN Charter, Articles 33–37 and 39–46.

12. UN Charter, Articles 10–17.

13. Stanley Meisler, *United Nations: The First Fifty Years* (Boston: Atlantic Monthly Press, 1997), 209.

14. Ibid., 211–212.

15. Ibid.

16. Ibid., 215. The "Zionism is racism" resolution stood until it was repealed in 1991, after the US-led victory in the Gulf War.

17. Jess Bravin and Steve Stecklow, "World Apart: UN Tackles a Changing Globe with Routines that Rarely Do," *Wall Street Journal*, December 16, 2003.

18. John Zaracostas, "U.N. control of Web rejected; Third World eyed regulation," *Washington Times*, December 8, 2003.

19. Meisler, 220.

20. Steven F. Hayward, *The Real Jimmy Carter* (Washington, D.C.: Regnery, 2004), 116.

21. Margaret Thatcher, *The Downing Street Years* (New York: HarperCollins, 1993), 182.

22. Meisler, 260–261.

CHAPTER EIGHT—CLINTON'S CLASSROOM

1. Margaret Thatcher, *The Downing Street Years* (New York: HarperCollins, 1993), 819.

2. http://www.jfklibrary.org/clinton_un_address.html.

3. Ibid. The reference to airports and airplanes is most curious, given the events of September 11, 2001. What did President Clinton know, when did he know it, and how did he act on the information? Did that information eve get passed along to President Bush and his administration?

4. Stanley Meisler, *United Nations: The First Fifty Years* (Boston: Atlantic Monthly Press, 1997), 299–300.

5. Ibid., 302–303.

6. Mark Bowden, *Black Hawk Down* (New York: Penguin, 2000), 72.

7. Ibid., 340–341.

8. Meisler, 308.
9. A senior naval officer told me that one result of the burdens Clinton imposed—social experiments, the UN deployments, the whole litany—was that about 50 percent of the commissioned officers in the Navy SEALs— among the best and most highly motivated troops we have—resigned rather than serve in Clinton's military.

CHAPTER NINE—UN REFORM: A FOOL'S ERRAND

1. UN press release, November 4, 2003.
2. Max Kampelman, "A Caucus of Democracies," *Wall Street Journal*, January 6, 2004.
3. UN Charter, Article 108.
4. Chirac speech to UN Security Council, *New York Times*, September 23, 2003.
5. Ibid.
6. Jesse Helms, "Saving the UN: A Challenge to the Next Secretary-General," *Foreign Affairs*, September–October 1996.
7. Speech by Lady Thatcher to The Atlantic Bridge, May 14, 2003, *The Times* (London), May 15, 2003.
8. "Views of a Changing World June 2003," Pew Research Center for the People and the Press, 27.
9. UN Charter, Article 97.
10. Chemical and biological weapons are not "weapons of mass destruction." They are area-denial weapons that kill people and deny the use of territory. The only weapons of mass destruction so far devised are nuclear weapons.
11. Reuters, March 15, 2004.

CHAPTER TEN—THE DEATH OF OLD EUROPE

1. Arnaud de Borchgrave, "Czech warns Europe of 'dream world' woes; President predicts EU problems," *Washington Times*, November 25, 2003.
2. Marc Miles, Edwin Feulner, Mary O'Grady, and Ana Eiras, *Index of Ec nomic Freedom* (Washington, D.C.: Heritage Foundation, 2004).
3. Ibid., 183.
4. Ibid., 191.
5. Ibid., 235.
6. Ibid., 103.
7. Ibid., 161.
8. BBC News, January 17, 2004.
9. Jean-Francois Revel, "Europe's Anti-American Obsession," *American Ente prise* magazine, December 2003.
10. FDR Fireside Chat to the Nation, September 11, 1941. http://www.usmm. org/fdr/ rattlesnake.html.
11. EU press release, December 10, 2003.
12. He held both positions from 2000 to 2003.

13. Nicholas Wapshott, Philip Webster, and David Charter, "Cherie said Bush 'stole' power and tackled him on executions," *London Times*, January 24, 2004.

14. An Article 32 investigation under the Uniform Code of Military Justice is the military equivalent of a grand jury hearing.

15. BBC News, June 3, 2003.

16. John J. Pershing, *My Experiences in the World War* (New York: Stokes, 1931), Vol. 1, 66–67.

17. A. B. C. Whipple, *To the Shores of Tripoli: The Birth of the U.S. Navy and Marines* (New York: William Morrow, 1991), 32

18. Ibid., 65.

CHAPTER ELEVEN—THE *EUNUCHS* AND THEIR UNION

1. George MacDonald Fraser, *Flashman and the Mountain of Light* (New York: Penguin, 1990), 287.

2. Though the idea for the EU is credited to a speech in 1950 by French foreign minister Robert Schuman, some polemicists have pointed out that the concept was outlined in considerable detail twenty-five years earlier by a then insignificant politician named Adolf Hitler in his notorious screed, *Mein Kampf.*

3. In 2003, the French government tried to outlaw the term "e-mail" because it wasn't French. They were too late to do anything about "spam." The canned spiced ham had fed too many starving Frenchmen during World War II, thanks to those reckless American cowboys who dropped tons of it off on their way to Berlin. It's better than snails and eels, no matter how much garlic you put on them.

4. *Hardball with Chris Matthews*, January 30, 2003. That quote has since been mis-attributed to everyone from Norman Schwartzkopf to Ross Perot. See Jim Beamguard, "Was It Something We Said?" *Tampa Tribune*, June 1, 2003.

5. Philip Delves Broughton and David Rennie, "Indignant French deny opposing a US victory," *Daily Telegraph*, March 29, 2003.

6. *Wall Street Journal*, December 2, 2003.

7. Ibid.

8. Ibid.

9. "World Briefing Europe: Europe May Lift Ban On Arms Sales To China," *New York Times*, January 27, 2004.

10. Ibid.

11. *Daily Telegraph*, February 18, 2003.

12. Source: CountryWatch.org.

13. "On the brink of a constitutional crisis: The EU should change the stability pact—not breach it," *Financial Times*, November 26, 2003.

14. Bruce Johnston, "EU pays pounds 1m to train Italian TV showgirls at 'school for bimbos'," *Daily Telegraph*, October 12, 2003.

15. Ambrose Evans-Pritchard, "EU auditors blast budget failings," *Daily Telegraph*, November 18, 2003.
16. *Daily Telegraph*, December 18, 2003; BBC News, December 16, 2003. It's not as good a deal as the UN bureaucrats have. The EUnuchs live in Brussels, not New York.
17. Version pending January 2004.
18. Article 13 attempts to reserve some power over economic and social issues to the member states by characterizing them as "shared competencies" with the EU. The inconsistency with other provisions of the EU draft seems to resolve the questions of power over these matters in favor of the EU, not the members.
19. BBC News, January 6, 2004.
20. Ibid.
21. Toby Helm and Ambrose Evans-Pritchard, "Blair calls for a quick deal on EU constitution," *Daily Telegraph*, March 26, 2004.

CHAPTER TWELVE—NATO AND THE *EU*NUCH MILITARY

1. Adam Smith, "The Wealth of Nations," 1776.
2. Ambrose Evans-Pritchard and Toby Helm, "France and Germany plan Euro defence union," *Daily Telegraph*, November 27, 2002.
3. Ibid.
4. Reuters Newsdesk, January 18, 2004.
5. Ibid.
6. *Daily Telegraph*, June 12, 2001.
7. Burridge, incidentally, was the British National Contingent Commander in the Iraq campaign of 2003.
8. AP News, March 11, 2004.
9. Elaine Sciolino and Lizette Alvarez, "Video Claims Al Qaeda Set Blasts in Spain; Officials Arrest 3 Moroccans and 2 Indians," *New York Times*, March 14, 2004.
10. *Al-Jazeera.net*, March 15, 2004.
11. Moore took great care to credit the Australian forces, who were, he said, "very, very good."

CHAPTER THIRTEEN—FORWARD TOGETHER, OR NOT

1. Stanley Meisler, *The United Nations: The First Fifty Years* (Boston: Atlantic Monthly Press, 1997), 35.

INDEX